What people are saying about …

FINDING GOD IN THE RUINS

"In *Finding God in the Ruins* we are given a unique gift, a rare invitation to listen to a hauntingly beautiful story where the darkest experiences of a person's life are redeemed. While he wields the sensibilities of an artist and the words of a poet, Matt bluntly exposes the beauty buried in the brokenness of the world. Be prepared. This isn't a book about clichés, easy answers, or simple faith. *Finding God in the Ruins* is a tenacious, relentless, and courageous pursuit of redemption that doesn't go around the pain, hoping to get by with less heartache by tenderly skirting the edges of a wound. Rather, Matt takes us on a deep dive right into the heart of pain where, surprisingly, we find ourselves in the heart of God."

Nate Pyle, pastor, blogger, and author of *Man Enough: How Jesus Redefines Manhood*

"Gritty, raw, vulnerable, and even at times uncomfortable, *Finding God in the Ruins* tackles the pain and brokenness of this world with the kind of compassion that lifts the veil of shame, allowing God to expose himself to the heart of humanity. Matt Bays is a brave soul who isn't afraid to search, to question God, and to sit with you in your pain as you slowly, gently, find yourself wrapped in the arms of a God who loves you beyond what you ever thought possible."

Logan Wolfram, author of *Curious Faith*, speaker, CEO of Allume

"A father with a sick son in need of healing said to Jesus, 'I do believe, help me with my unbelief.' Often the journey to believe begins with an honest confession of unbelief. Honest, not fake. If you struggle with God, have a ton of questions, have no time for cliché answers, but still long for hope, you are going to thoroughly enjoy the journey Matt Bays is taking you on through his own story. If you like things neat, tidy, and orderly, don't you dare turn to the next page."

Randy Frazee, author *of Think, Act, Be Like Jesus* and *The Heart of the Story*

"Chock-full of wisdom and insight, Matt Bays delivers a deeply moving account of pain, doubt, and ultimately hope. Bays delivers his powerful message with wisdom, humility, and heart. I am certain his stories will stay with me long after I've turned the last page. Powerful. Deeply human. Unforgettable."

Lori Nelson Spielman, bestselling author of *The Life List* and *Sweet Forgiveness*; www.lorinelsonspielman.com

"Matt Bays has written an insightful narrative that explores the biblical metaphor of redemption. While rejecting a simplistic salvation that promises peace and prosperity to all who believe, the author explores human suffering from the biblical idea that the God who took on flesh enters into human suffering and redeems it. Through personal stories, Matt Bays invites the reader to explore a theodicy that is critical but compassionate. His is a real and refreshing invitation to allow our stories to speak words of hope to fellow strugglers. I recommend this book for both personal and group study."

David Sebastian, dean emeritus at
Anderson University School of Theology

"Matt Bays knows about pain and suffering, and writes about it with the raw transparency of someone who has experienced deep loss. But this book exhales genuine hope on every page, pointing to the expansive God who sits with us when we are lost, weeping with us and helping us to finally find our feet again. If you are sitting in the midst of failure and loss, pick up this book and find the God who is already there with you."

Steve Wiens, author of *Beginnings*

"*Finding God in the Ruins* will make some readers shift in their chairs. I expect some will be tempted to scoot back from the table and leave just as the conversation gets going. I think that's a good sign. This book is for people who have been afraid to tell the truth, afraid to look a painful past in the eye, afraid to speak uncertainties about God, and afraid they might be right about their unworthiness. By laying his own painful story plainly in the light, Matt is going first and making space for us to lay our own stories right there beside his. His writing is both powerfully poetic and accessible, and will make you laugh and cry in succession. *Finding God in the Ruins* is the start of a desperately needed conversation, giving believers and unbelievers alike permission to be real and to be on the lookout for hope and redemption in unlikely places."

Christa Wells, GMA Dove Award–
winning songwriter of the year

"*Finding God in the Ruins* is raw, honest, and hopeful. A heartbreakingly beautiful story that shows us a new and interesting perspective on elements of faith and our relationship with Jesus."

Jon McLaughlin, songwriter/recording artist

"With rare vulnerability, wounded healer Matt Bays offers compelling evidence of the importance of reclaiming our stories. Heartrending vignettes offer insight into the certainty that although we may never find answers to the 'whys' of our wretchedness, we will find God there in the ruins."

Amy K. Sorrells, survivor advocate and award-winning author of the novels *How Sweet the Sound, Then Sings My Soul,* and *Lead Me Home*

FINDING

GOD

IN THE

RUINS

FINDING

GOD

IN THE

RUINS

How God Redeems Pain

MATT BAYS

David C Cook®
transforming lives together

FINDING GOD IN THE RUINS
Published by David C Cook
4050 Lee Vance View
Colorado Springs, CO 80918 U.S.A.

David C Cook Distribution Canada
55 Woodslee Avenue, Paris, Ontario, Canada N3L 3E5

David C Cook U.K., Kingsway Communications
Eastbourne, East Sussex BN23 6NT, England

The graphic circle C logo is a registered trademark of David C Cook.

The website addresses recommended throughout this book are offered as a
resource to you. These websites are not intended in any way to be or imply an
endorsement on the part of David C Cook, nor do we vouch for their content.

Unless otherwise noted, all Scripture quotations are taken from the Holy Bible, NEW
INTERNATIONAL VERSION®, NIV®. Copyright © 1973, 2011 by Biblica, Inc.® Used
by permission. All rights reserved worldwide. NEW INTERNATIONAL VERSION® and
NIV® are registered trademarks of Biblica, Inc. Use of either trademark for the offering of
goods or services requires the prior written consent of Biblica, Inc. Scripture quotations
marked ASV are taken from the American Standard Version. (Public Domain.); ESV are
taken from the ESV® Bible (The Holy Bible, English Standard Version®), copyright © 2001
by Crossway, a publishing ministry of Good News Publishers. Used by permission. All
rights reserved; KJV are taken from the King James Version of the Bible. (Public Domain.);
TLB are taken from The Living Bible, copyright © 1971. Used by permission of Tyndale
House Publishers, Inc., Carol Stream, Illinois 60188. All rights reserved; THE MESSAGE are
taken from THE MESSAGE. Copyright © by Eugene H. Peterson 1993, 2002. Used by
permission of Tyndale House Publishers, Inc; NIV 1984 are taken from the Holy Bible, New
International Version®, NIV®. Copyright © 1973, 2011 by Biblica, Inc.™ Used by permission
of Zondervan. All rights reserved worldwide. www.zondervan.com; NKJV are taken from
the New King James Version®. Copyright © 1982 by Thomas Nelson. Used by permission.
All rights reserved. The author has added italics to Scripture quotations for emphasis.

LCCN 2015953187
ISBN 978-0-7814-1383-1
eISBN 978-0-7814-1425-8

© 2016 Matt Bays

The Team: Tim Peterson, Nick Lee, Cara Iverson, Helen Macdonald, Susan Murdock
Cover Design: Amy Konyndyk
Cover Photo: Getty Images and iStockphoto

Printed in the United States of America
First Edition 2016

1 2 3 4 5 6 7 8 9 10

010516

For Wee

CONTENTS

I form the light and create darkness, I bring prosperity and create disaster; I, the LORD, *do all these things.*

—Isaiah 45:7

PREFACE

God, in real life, is nothing like the God we've been taught about in church. Anyone who has been through tragedy, pain, trauma, or devastating loss knows that in those moments, and in the terrible aftermath, hell often feels much more powerful than heaven.

In the midst of suffering, we find ourselves trying to bear the absence of God, sometimes while doubting his very existence. And although those around us think they have the answers, their well-intentioned words often translate as cruel and useless. What if we aren't going to "get better"? What if our sufferings and doubt are necessary components—or even the very essence of our faith?

Perhaps you are troubled by how much heartbreak and catastrophe is in the world. Perhaps you struggle to understand a God who allows such shocking personal tragedy and pointless suffering.

I get it. All hell broke loose in my life shortly after I was born in 1970. I spent years trying to make sense of God's "higher ways" but was told to be careful, that my questions could drive me away from my faith altogether. But doubt is part of life, and our faith can be strengthened when we increase our understanding of who God *really* is by allowing ourselves to ask the difficult questions.

By reading this book, I hope you will discover that not everything must be redeemed the way it was promised to you. There will be no pressure to find an answer or spiritual cliché that will pull you or anyone else back together. There will be no silver linings or theological formulations of how all things work together for the *real* good. I simply want to come alongside you in your trouble—in the pain and suffering of your loved ones for whom answers have not yet come, and in your wrestling over the kind of God who has left so many in this world waiting on their redemption.

Together, I want to see if we might find God sitting in the ruins of our lives, shaking his head, same as us, over all that has happened.

ACKNOWLEDGMENTS

Kathy Helmers—I knew something like this would only be possible if someone like you was out there. And there you were. Thank you for your generous investment in my growth as a writer, and for your extraordinary insight on this project from the ground up. But I especially thank you for always asking about Trina. Every single time. *Me encanta.*

Carin Cryderman—for tearing apart early drafts and being willing to call foul every time I wasn't honest.

The team at David C. Cook—Tim Peterson, a huge thank-you for understanding what this is all about. Also, Tim Close, Ingrid Beck, Darren Terpstra, Marilyn Largent, Amy Konyndyk, Annette Brickbealer, Chriscynethia Floyd, Helen Macdonald, Lisa Beech, Karla Colonnieves, Alice Crider, and Andy Meiscnheimer. You are all gifted people with beautiful hearts. I can't thank you enough.

Brian Edwards—you're a godsend and my brother.

Doug the Counselor—for being fluent in the language of life.

Andrea McCaffrey—for cheerleading every step of the way.

Jason Coons—for bringing levity into my life.

Jeff Korbini—for praying on your dog walks.

Garrett Edwards—for saying, "Wounds need air." The world needs you, man. Keep going.

Angela DeVon Hunt—for your beautiful penmanship.

Mom—for knowing I could do anything.

Trina (Wee)—my sister, war vet, and best friend. You ARE kind of a big deal. Call me.

Chloe and Evalee—I'm so grateful for the strong women you already are. You are my family. I couldn't be more proud of you.

Heather—you have always seen me as the man I'm still not sure I actually am. I've needed someone to do that. Thank you. Caring and complex, courageous and loyal, stunning, wise, serious, honest, and real. You're not like anyone.

God—for balancing the dark with so many beautiful things. And for making the dark beautiful in its own way.

And finally, to whoever reads this book—let the healing begin.

PART 1

THE BACKSTORY

THE PEN
Where Is God?

I used to say, "His ways are higher," but by higher I meant better.

Tim and Janese were sitting in the same two seats they sat in every Sunday at church. For years I had heard them sing such words as "Oh my God, he will not delay," "Your grace is enough," "You never let go, through the calm and through the storm." But on this particular weekend, I avoided their gaze. I was broken by their recent tragedy, and it felt cruel to sing these words—to sing at all in their presence.

One week earlier their son had thrown a piece of rope over a beam of wood and hung himself in his garage. But still their eyes were closed tightly and tears streamed down their faces as they sang, "Bless the Lord, O my soul, O my soul … I'll worship his holy name."

I thought about the song lyricists. When they picked up their pens to write these words, promises that millions of people around the world would sing each weekend, were they taking into consideration only the people who were in fairly good shape, whose lives were firing on all cylinders, or were they including people like Tim and Janese?

When I could no longer ignore their pain, I focused all my attention their way. I sang with them as if we were the only three people in the room, but I couldn't stop wondering how they were still out there after all they had been through.

Tim and Janese would say that once someone loses a child to suicide (or loses a child at all), life is never the same. But they would also tell you that God is the same.

I have needed the honest presence of people like Tim and Janese in my life. When I was in my twenties, fresh out of college and hot off the clergy presses, I had no knowledge of what I was doing, nor any idea of what "God's grace is enough" actually meant.

During my first week as a professional pastor, I was asked to visit a woman whose husband didn't make it through a routine angioplasty. On my way to the hospital, I felt some sort of God-pressure to give explanations to this woman who would be going home without the love of her life. I knew what I was supposed to say to her: "All things work together for the good of those who love God" (see Rom. 8:28).

But saying those words made me feel like a fraud, and I knew I was the wrong man for the job. I felt like a 350-pound jockey at the Kentucky Derby with no business being on that horse. All those classes and all that training and I was still ill equipped for the job.

On my way home from the hospital, I realized I would never be capable of healing someone completely. And if not completely, what was the point? I had been armed with simplistic and defective answers for obliterating people's pain, but my word-bombs were always detonating at the wrong time. It would be years before I found the confidence to try a less religious approach: the approach of simply being present.

For many years in my own search for redemption, I needed others to be the hands of God to me—to let me know that if things didn't work out, they would stand with me, even if I stopped believing.

Most of my spiritual mentors never said the words I was desperate to hear: "I'm so sorry for all you are going through. You are going to make it, and I'm going to be there for you if you need me. You don't need to be anything other than what you are in this moment." Instead I heard only this substandard spiritual remedy: "God has a plan, and one day he will use this for his glory, so get on with it."

My brokenness for God's glory. It felt like a slap in the face. I could not bear the responsibility for making sure my pain would eventually be turned into something that would make God look good. What I really needed to know was that in spite of my pain, I would be okay, even if things never got turned around.

If I were God, I would travel back in time to 1982 to the fat, dirty man who sat at the ice cream stand every Sunday night after church, muttering, "Schizophrenia, schizo! Something's wrong in here." Even as an eleven-year-old boy, I thought this was meaningless. And if I were God, I would have taken that man's head in my hands, gazed into his eyes until he saw me, and with one loving look set him free. From that day forward, he would've stood up straight, washed his hair, gotten a job, gotten married, had a couple of kids, and coached his kids' Little League baseball team. And instead of dying alone and schizophrenic, he would've been surrounded by his loved ones when he was old and gray as he peacefully drifted into the arms of God.

It seems that it would be simple to fix things. Trust me, I get it. It seems as though a person could be born whole and then ride out life without the unnecessary trials and complications.

I used to pray that the unredeemed circumstances in my life would be made right. But then my older brother died after living just twenty-three years of an extremely troubled life, and my sister's breast cancer came out of remission with a vengeance, spreading throughout her body like wildfire. And me? I was raised by wolves. What happened in the privacy of our home when I was just a boy would eventually catch up with me and confiscate my faith altogether.

But as it turned out, that confiscation would be exactly what I needed. Because I have found out something about God that I cannot undo. God is not who I thought he was—not who I was *told* he was.

———

Christianity has become so precise over the years—an exacting science with ever more complicated mathematical promises. Perhaps you have noticed this. You might have brought up some very reasonable questions to "the faithful" but were told to put your questions away or classified as "oh ye of little faith."

Much of our time with God, personally or corporately within the church structure, has been spent trying to get something: healing, money, the so-called desires of our hearts. We've been looking for a hallelujah, and when we didn't get it we assumed it was because we didn't have enough faith or pray the right prayer.

We have created redemption from a hand-me-down God and forced ourselves into believing that all things work together for the good, turning this promise into an empty cliché that might or might not have come true for us the way we understood it. And often when it didn't come true, our misguided understanding of redemption left us believing we should have been able to overcome our pain with mind control.

No wonder we pressure others to "get better" or "learn to depend on God." Maybe we should consider the possibility that we haven't been put in their lives to help *them* get healed. Maybe, in fact, the reverse could be true: that they are God's gift to us, showing us how to grieve, how to plumb the depths of hell and survive, and how to find grace.

But we have little patience for survival that looks like depression, despair, or unbelief, because if we allow others unbelief, we have to allow ourselves unbelief. If we allow others despair, we realize that we ourselves could also despair. And we're not sure we can handle looking that closely at our pain.

Or maybe we simply don't know what it is to lose a child or be full of cancer or be beaten or cheated on by the person who promised to love, honor, and cherish us. And if that's true, we must listen rather than presume. We must invite others to tell us their stories and then listen to them, hear them, feel them, and play out each awful scene in our mind, taking a deep breath before we ever say a word. We must struggle to understand what it was like for them, how it split their world in two, what we would need if *their* story were *our* story.

They need hearts filled with empathy, not mouths filled with *our* take on *their* story. Standing alongside someone in silent compassion is powerful.

But it's nearly impossible to offer the kind of compassion they will need when their story doesn't fit into the distorted view of redemption we continue to believe in and hold to.

The truth is, redemption has been misunderstood. Modern Christianity has defined it this way:

> **Redemption** (rĭ-dĕmp′shən) *n.*—A state of existence in which the faithful to God receive what they expect to receive out of life (and out of God), and what ails them is converted into something fresh and new. (Getting the desires of one's heart.)[1]

Several years ago I watched a Christian movie about a high school sports team and their coach who were facing several battles, including a string of game losses, parental disrespect, a malfunctioning car, and infertility. They prayed for help, and boy did they get it: everything they asked for and more. The team broke their losing streak and won every game that season, including the championship. The disrespect for their parents melted away. The school purchased a brand-new truck to replace the coach's clunker. And if all this wasn't enough to get audiences on their feet and cheering for God, by the end of the movie, the coach's wife was pregnant.

I sat in my living room disheartened by how easily all their wishes had come true while one of my closest friends and his wife, who had loved God since they were teenagers, had suffered through seven miscarriages.

When this caricature of redemption becomes the hallmark of our faith, it creates a real problem for us and for others. It becomes difficult to approach God outside the context of getting what we want, which leads to either disillusionment with God or a petty and shallow faith experience. When God doesn't wipe the slate clean for us or a problem lingers too long, we begin writing our own version of Christianity, pretending that solutions are simple, black and white, or based on our good works and faithful prayers rather than God's grace. To others, this dumbing down of our faith is either an overexposed snapshot of God, with very little contrast, or an underdeveloped Polaroid that doesn't look a thing like God. And it is one of the main reasons Christians come across as out of touch, irrelevant, or even cruel to the rest of the world.

We might not be able to fully admit it yet, but deep down many of us believe that God owes us. We think that because we are chosen, God should deliver. As children, many of us memorized such verses as Psalm 37:5: "Commit thy way unto the LORD; trust also in him; and he shall bring it to pass" (KJV). But when things don't come to pass, we feel tricked. To us, his promise of redemption, to give us a good life, is a transacted agreement with his signature on the dotted line, and he needs to either pay up or be sent to collections.

We think of the word *redeemed* and imagine the removal of pain. We see something broken in our lives or in the lives of others and envision it getting fixed within a certain time frame: "Dear God,

please take this away ... or that away ... help me do this ... or stop
doing that ... please make this or that happen for me, us, them." But
things do not always work out, do they? In fact, incredibly important
things do not always work out. People get cancer or give birth to
babies with no capacity for brain development; they put a bullet in
their head when they can no longer see themselves in this world, or
they unknowingly stumble upon an addiction, and the best years of
their lives are rung out like a washrag.

And so it seems that the very word *redeemed* needs its own personal redemption.

I will be using the word *unredeemed* to refer to a particular category of
people or to clarify a situation or life circumstance that hasn't fallen
in line with our traditional understanding of the word *redemption*—
meaning, it didn't get healed, it didn't go away, they didn't find the
bit of goodness in it that they had expected, and they certainly didn't
find God in the ruins.

The unredeemed are those whose lives have been neither helped
nor healed by the usual spiritual remedies. They have experienced
great loss and continue to experience the residual pain of despair.
Their promise of redemption seems far into the future—far away
from the here and now. Their pain is not going away anytime soon,
perhaps not ever.

They have lost children, endure chronic illness, are neglected
or abused, have experienced an atrocity, suffer from mental illness,
or struggle against a nameless woe. Frequently their sufferings are

irreversible or the sins that have come against them have left a scar that will permanently disfigure a part of their lives.

So, then, who are the redeemed?

Contrary to what we've been told, redemption is not an escape but rather a journey. We've been programmed to expect redemption without a lot of prep work. But redemption will always be most powerful when we can trace God's hand along the way. A lightning-bolt miracle is not so impressive to me these days, but looking back to see where God's hands have pushed the clay of brokenness into something we never thought it could become is truly redemptive.

That said, the redeemed are those who acknowledge to the best of their ability the harsh reality of their broken story, who accept that while their pain does not define them, it does define the power of their redemption. They have somehow managed to find God in the ruins, sitting in the midst of their personal hell even when God wasn't healing one infernal thing. The redeemed have the capacity to be *reasonably* happy despite their pain and allow God to use their brokenness for good, creating a much deeper sense of self, purpose, and meaning for their lives.

But to find our redemption, we must be willing to visit the scene of the crime and, unimaginably, stay there for a while. It will take some time to survey the damage, to sit in the ruins with God and acknowledge its full impact on our lives. But if we are ever to take our power back, this necessary evil must be part of our journey.

I have often felt that the pain of tragedy, abuse, or great loss is like a bad hitchhiker who has taken over the driver's seat of our lives and careened us off into the woods. And I believe if we are to keep from being overwhelmed by it, we can't pretend it didn't drive us to an uninhabited location and violate us by the side of the road. We might never fully dispel the pain of that experience, but that is not our goal. Our goal is to diffuse the pain—to get it out of the driver's seat and convince it to ride shotgun so that we can enjoy life again.

It's up to us.

We can continue waiting for lightning to strike or pretend that it has and we've been cured, or we can begin the journey to finding true redemption and, with it, a deeper purpose for our lives as we come to understand, or maybe just accept, how God redeems pain.

Becky and I were coworkers. She was a bright spot in my workday. She loved cats, and if someone didn't, she would torment the person by putting photos in his or her office mailbox of tiny kittens sitting in baskets or playing with balls of yarn. She was a total prankster, and you could always tell when she was up to something because she would begin talking through her teeth. To most of us, Becky seemed happy. But then one morning, Becky's great sorrow—her pain, desperation, fear, and despair—gathered around her bed and told her that her time was up. And she believed it. Shortly after her husband, John, had gone off to work, she filled her gut with pills and was gone before he arrived home.

On a Wednesday evening, I stepped outside on my front porch to take a call from a staff member from my church. "She's gone," he said, and that was all. He started to say more, but his voice quivered and stopped working. After our phone call I stepped back inside and quietly watched as my daughters made their evening preparations for the next day. We spoke about school stuff, yet I have no recollection of our words. My wife, Heather, sat in a chair close by and stared at me. She knew something was up.

The next morning our staff gathered in a small chapel on our campus to talk about what had happened to Becky. Some looked terribly sad, while others hid their anger by staring at their knees. When someone dies suddenly, it takes time to accept the loss. When someone dies tragically, we plod through, wishing things would've been different, but in time we come to accept our lives without them. But when someone takes their own life, those of us left in the afterkill wait for an answer to a question we never asked. And without answers, we either lumber around like zombies in an old movie or change the channel to a cooking show.

I spent time that afternoon processing in my journal:

Today I write for a friend who lost her fight with the great depression. I sat with thirty colleagues who loved her—we sat arm in arm waiting for someone to tell us something that would make sense of it. The only man who spoke told us, as tears ran down his face, that his father had taken his life seventeen years earlier. He told us his dad didn't know how to make life work and that was all he knew. Our tears flowed, cleansing something terribly sad within us.

One year earlier, Becky had already tried with a handful of pills to stop the world from spinning madly on. She must've been so tired.

"The heart has its reasons which reason knows nothing of"—Blaise Pascal.

I wonder if she cried as she wrote her final words. I can't imagine she felt worthy as she spelled out the reasons her life was no longer worth living. I hope they saved the pen she used—that the leftover ink inside will be used only to write words of love and hope and that after ten thousand love notes, a balance will be found and she will be at peace.

She loved her cats as children. I wonder if they knew what she was up to as they watched her take a larger handful of pills this time. I wonder if she felt relieved as the pills disintegrated in the soul of her belly—as they took her to places of good memories, love, and laughter before she drifted away. I hope the first face she saw was the face of God and that she heard his voice telling her all the things she never believed about herself.

I hope she flew so lightly into the clouds with her eyes shut, with her red hair blowing. She was so beautiful. And lonely. And loved.

I'm sorry I didn't see more, Becky, and I promise to learn from this, to go with my gut, to continue looking for the broken and promising them that everything will be okay.

I will miss your political jabs on Facebook, at anything even slightly left. I will miss your standing in the front row of my choir and how you so terribly wanted to raise your hands in worship but felt conspicuous. I will miss how I almost never saw you without a smile on your face. I will miss your talking through your teeth. I will miss seeing your car in the parking lot with "Becky the Cat Sitter" scrolled across the windows. I will miss your love of the little things. I will miss you, Becky. We all will. Madly.

In 1992, several months after my brother Tim was involved in a fatal motorcycle accident, I received a letter from a friend of a friend. She had spent the summer with Tim at a campground in West Virginia and wrote to me of all the great things she had seen in him while they were there. I read her letter at least twenty-five times and was grateful she had sent it. It would've been easy for her to write the letter and toss it aside, thinking it wouldn't have been meaningful to me because she and I didn't know each other well. But it was meaningful, and twenty-two years later I still have her letter.

Thinking back on that letter encouraged me to send my journal entry about Becky off to John (Becky's husband). I received a very short reply that evening that said thank you and little else. I wondered if my actions were impulsive; I hoped I hadn't slammed him with a hard dose of reality before it was time. I worried that my words might have done just that.

Several days later when I walked into our church's auditorium for Becky's funeral, I saw John down front, standing over her. It was the first time I felt anger for what she had done. I thought to myself, *Was this really what she wanted? To be lying dead in a church?* I could see her bright red hair creeping over the top of the casket that held her. John stood there, probably wondering impossibly about what he could have done to be more, love more, *see* more.

The whole scene was too much for me, so I headed to my office to prepare the songs I would be singing during her service. By the time I came back to the auditorium, at least a hundred people stood in line to speak to John. I watched him hug each person, his tall frame hulking over the women, which he was used to because Becky was barely five feet tall. Each time I saw him break down in someone's arms, I felt agitated: *How could she have done this to him?* My anger intensified.

When I finally reached the front of the line, for a brief moment his face lit up. "I have something for you," he said, but his smile quickly faded and his eyes filled with tears as he reached into his pocket. "I want you to have this." He pulled a pen from his pocket and placed it in my hand. I knew instantly. It was Becky's pen—the pen she had used to scrawl her final words. I thought about the journal entry I had sent him: "I hope they saved the pen she used—that the leftover ink inside will be used only to write words of love and hope."

"I know you like to write, Matt," he said to me, "so please write beautiful, hope-filled words with this pen." Tears replaced the anger as I made a silent promise to use Becky's pen only to write words of love and hope to people going through unbearable difficulties—and to use it this way until I had drained it dry.

Write beautiful, hope-filled words.

I'll do my best, John.

This is how my journey began.

ONE-SIDED PRAYERS
It's Not Adding Up

The greatest and most important problems of life are all fundamentally insoluble. They can never be solved but only outgrown.

—Carl Jung

I was just six years old. I was sitting on a small love seat in our family room on Hemlock Drive shortly after my mom's second husband had emotionally sacked our home, beaten her up, taken his keys, and driven off in a fit of rage. I brushed her hair and listened to her cry. I wanted to fix her life. I wanted to make things better for her, but I was six years old. So instead I brushed her hair and asked God to make things better for her.

My gut response to brokenness, even at six years old, was to call out to God—to pray. But I was already beginning to understand that not all my prayers got answered.

The most unread pages of my Bible are toward the back. The book of Revelation reads more like a sci-fi novel than an ancient

God-story, and most of the people I know ignore Revelation alto-gether because they don't know what to do with it. Neither do I.

I've never liked sci-fi. When I was a kid, my mom had to wake me up at the end of *Star Wars* because it had literally bored me to sleep. I was hoping to see *Herbie Goes to Monte Carlo* because at that age, who doesn't love seeing a Volkswagen riding around causing trouble?

The imagery in Revelation never has been easily accessible to me, but then one day I happened upon a word picture from the fifth chapter that fully caught my attention:

> [They] fell down before the Lamb. Each one had
> a harp and they were holding golden bowls full of
> incense, which are the prayers of God's people. (v. 8)

I can see these bowls in my mind, filled with incense, with prayers that had been left before God, piled high and teeming with our needs. What requests had been made? What desires had been col-lected in these gold bowls, and why hadn't they been sorted through yet? I wondered who had prayed them and if mine were a part of this collection. I was fascinated at the thought of God collecting and saving our prayers.

This idea of an accumulation of prayers stacked in bowls and sitting somewhere in heaven has never left me, and I'm not alone. It turns out that scholars are also bothered and delighted by this verse and have taken stabs at what it means. Some conjure up scenes of *Gladiator* meets *Avatar*, reminding me again why I've never read from Revelation. But others keep it simple. They believe that every prayer ever prayed is in one of the bowls—that God is a hoarder and likes prayers most of all.

But I wasn't satisfied just yet, so I continued my search.

I rummaged online and in commentaries. Each resource offered multiple thoughts, but one theory was represented by nearly every source I looked into. Unanswered prayers. Many theologians believe that the gold bowls are filled with one-sided prayers that have been prayed but left unanswered.

Is this true? Is God collecting our unanswered prayers? I imagine the prayers of millions of people: "Save me," "Deliver me," "Heal me," "Love me," "Fix me," "Use me," "Feed me," "Release me," "Have me," "Hold me," "Fill me," "Take me," "Sustain me," "Liberate me," "Rescue me," "Come through for me," "*Redeem* me."

I feel the desperation of such words as *cancer, sexual brokenness, alone, bastard, abused, diseased, disillusioned,* and *unloved* and that each one has been turned into a ruined potpourri and poured into these golden bowls as an offering unto God. How can it not burn God's nostrils? How can it not cause God to cough and wheeze and realize that he must act quickly and answer the prayers of the unredeemed?

If I were God, I would respond to the unredeemed. I would wake up their murdered children and pull their cancer out by the roots. The sweet aroma from the incense of life, love, and healing would permeate the air, not the stench found among the wreckage of divorce, disease, suicide, abuse, and death.

And as for the abuses that have created a panic room in my heart, I'd show up in person, because although some unredeemed *things* need fixing, unredeemed *people* need proximity, comfort, to be touched, held, loved.

Over the years, I've told people things about God that were simply not true. I've turned good rules into bad rules by using them at the wrong time and place, and a rule applied out of context can be so incredibly destructive.

I would love to be able to make some of the positive sayings and scriptures we use as spiritual loopholes actually work. "Everything happens for a reason" isn't destructive if your kid loses a piece of candy through the cracks of the bleachers or if your car stalls on the side of the road. But it can be very destructive if spoken when someone's biopsy comes back positive. "When God closes a door he opens a window" is fine for not getting that job you always wanted or for a blind date gone wrong. It doesn't work for divorce. It doesn't work for someone's kid not staying in rehab. And if someone is standing over their wife's lifeless body at a funeral, beautiful and powerful words such as "all things work together for our good" are poison in a pretty pill. Out of context, rules—even really good ones—make God look like Hitler.

Sometimes I feel that God should be going about the whole process differently. I find myself wanting to take over for him—to slide him into the copilot's seat and let him press the dummy buttons, twist knobs, and flip disconnected switches while I sit in the pilot's seat and get this thing in the air. There are times when I feel I'd do a better job of it all—that instead of skidding across the runway with our fingers crossed, we'd fly first-class, with no turbulence, our own personal flight attendant, and have a tour of the cockpit if we wanted. And this is when I've often been told that I just need to trust God.

But *why* trust him?

After Becky's funeral, I struggled with the injustice of John having to walk this road alone. I couldn't help but feel he had been abandoned, not only by Becky but also by God.

The older I've gotten, the greater my doubts have become, which is not something I feel the need to cure. The frustration we feel with God is fair, and I worry more about those who resist an honest doubt or two. As I've heard it said, unexpressed doubt can be toxic.

Opening my hands and allowing the spiritual clichés and wrongly applied Scripture verses to slip through my fingers was the beginning of my liberation from the simplistic and defective answers to life's most powerful and haunting questions. It initiated something within me that I couldn't stop and didn't want to stop.

I decided to set everything I had been told about God aside and let go of this old version of him I had carried around for decades. But no sooner had I started down this path than I realized letting go would be harder than I thought. It wouldn't be something I could fully settle on a weekend retreat or conference; it would be a process.

I would have to go back to where it all started because I had my own questions. I would have to revisit the past and all that had happened in my life to see if I could find the pleasure in the pain, the redemption among the thorns. I would need to get everything out on the table and reexamine all I had ever believed about God's plan to redeem us—to redeem me.

I had promised myself that I wouldn't feel the need to protect God. If things didn't work out in his favor, if he came off as a cheat and a liar, so be it. And I promised that at the end of this journey, when the dust settled, I'd let the chips fall where they would.

Certain my words wouldn't all be hope-filled, I got out my pen anyway and began to write my untold story.

This is the story of the unredeemed.

THE CHAIN
Kicking God Out of Your Life

Did anything happen when we got Jesus off the
streets and into our hearts? And if so, what did it
matter if nothing really changed in our lives?

I got "saved" on a dare.

Getting saved was expected of every man, woman, and child in my church of origin. This was the moment you invited Jesus to live in your heart because apparently he had been homeless while we were all out sinning. Getting saved made old ladies swoon and preachers feel useful. And of course there was only one way to do this: walk to the front of the room, kneel at an altar as if your life depended on it, and say, "I'm a sinner, so please come live inside my heart, Homeless Jesus."

I'm guessing my brother was nine and I was eight when we cooked up the scheme to walk down to the altar together. Tim, not nearly the sensitive kid I was, came up with the idea, and what had started as a harmless dare quickly became a "double-dare-ya" that I wished I hadn't sworn allegiance to. He was relentless when he wanted something, and when I couldn't take the begging anymore, I gave in.

Sunday finally came. While we turned ourselves into the world's youngest business leaders with our slacks and clip-on ties, he kept asking if I was really going to follow through with it.

"You're not gonna leave me hanging, are you?"

"No, Tim. If you go, I'll go," I kept telling him.

"Okay. I just want to make sure because I feel like you're planning to ditch me on the way down to the altar." It was an odd conversation to me, especially because I was never the one who backed out of our deals.

Sunday mornings at church had a certain rhythm—a predictable routine I was used to. First I would punch Uncle Zethre in the stomach as hard as I could, and he would stick his finger up in the air, pretending to feel for a breeze. Then I would shake a couple of the old people's worn-out hands, grab a bulletin so I could draw pictures during the service, and head to the sanctuary. But there was nothing predictable about this Sunday morning and I was nervous.

All the way in, Tim kept whispering, "You promise?"

"I already said 'I promise' a hundred times! What are you so worried about?"

I was agitated about getting saved because I didn't really know what I was getting saved from. I had a feeling it was from such things as looking at Mary Jane Brewster's underwear when I was in second grade or secretly hating Mrs. Hadaway in fourth.

All throughout the preaching, my heart raced. A part of me already loved God, although I had no idea how or even why. He'd never done that much for me outside of dying on a cross, which all seemed a little foolish and unnecessary. But somehow he still occupied an easy chair inside of me, and even at eight years old, I listened to him when he told me to be nice or tell the truth.

If there were fifty-two church services in a year, you would've been hard-pressed to tell one from the other, except for the Christmas service, because that's when they put out the poinsettias. Uncle Garnel (Zethre's little brother) was the pastor of our church. All his messages were the same, with a lot of yelling and finger-pointing and the word *flustrating* worked into every one. He was angry with kids these days who thought they could just drink and cuss and not have to answer for it. "Well, they *will* have to answer for it!" he'd tell us. "And it is so *flustrating*!"

My aunt Linda played the organ, and we all knew the end of the message was coming when she walked up front and sat down on the organ bench. (It was a family affair. My uncle played the piano, my great-uncle helped with the offering, and my great-aunt organized the all-church dinners.) I'm not sure how, but Aunt Linda always knew when things were winding down. She'd take off her high heels, push a few organ stoppers (which always fascinated me), and press her fingers into the keys, instantly making our church feel as though God had arrived.

Uncle Garnel would begin telling us that this was the day of our salvation. "If you wait, it just might be too late," he'd say. I liked the meter of it.

I looked around and saw an older lady's husband who had held out on getting saved for a lot longer than I had. "Please turn to page *blah-blah-blah*," the song leader would say. (He was my second cousin, seriously.) So we took out our hymnals and thumbed through the thick cream-colored pages until we found "Just As I Am."

For the next fifteen or twenty minutes, depending on how long it took for some of us to come forward for our saving, we would sing the same couple of verses over and over.

"Go now," Tim said.

"Let's wait until someone else goes first," I told him.

"No. Go now. You promised you would."

"I will!" I yelled in a whisper.

My mom hushed us.

Then Tim started pushing my back to get me into the aisle. I dug my unsaved fingernails into his arm. "Ouch! What is your problem?"

"You boys better knock it off right now," my mom whispered at us with one eye half-closed, which meant bad things for us when we got home.

I was still planning to go but was waiting for someone else to prime the pump. Finally some girl in skintight white pants walked past us. Her head was bowed perfectly, and it was perhaps the humblest walk I had ever seen. She was serious about her saving. Now it was my turn.

"You ready?" I asked my brother. I was terrified.

"Yes. I've been ready," he answered, not seeming a bit nervous. "Now, go. I'll be right behind you."

I took the tiniest step, just barely into the aisle. Tim took a step behind me. He was coming too, just like he'd promised. My mother gasped when she realized what was happening. She covered her mouth, overwhelmed that her two boys were getting saved.

Yes, finally. God is good, I imagined her saying.

I confidently took another step away from our family pew, placing myself solidly in the aisle now, where everyone could see. I looked behind me to gauge Tim's whereabouts, but he had stepped back to his seat. I whispered his name to get his attention, but his head was bowed and hands folded as if he were praying harder than he had ever prayed in his life. It was the most precious thing, and this is when I knew.

He wasn't coming. I was on my own.

Every eye in the place was on me. It was the reason so many of them came to church in the first place: an eight-year-old was getting saved. It thrilled the old ladies to have their prayers answered. I wanted to step back to my seat but was too far into the aisle to turn back. Hatred boiled inside of me. Tim was a filthy liar, and exactly how was I supposed to get saved with hatred in my heart *and* on a dare? I was on a bobsled straight to hell.

When I reached the end of the aisle, Uncle Garnel was waiting to pray me into God's good graces so I wouldn't suffer eternal conscious torture at the hands of the pitchforked, horned devil I saw on Saturday morning cartoons. I felt immense guilt when I knelt down to pray, expecting a tongue-lashing from Uncle Garnel for all I had done wrong in my eight reckless years. But to my surprise, he spoke as sweetly as I'd ever heard him speak. Most of his sermons were filled with anger and intolerance, but at the altar that day, I heard only love in his voice.

I don't know if the angels sang or I changed my eternal travel destination that day, but I do believe there was glory, whatever you believe that to be, and that God was reclining on that easy chair inside of me. As author Anne Lamott so eloquently put it, "So this was my beautiful moment of conversion."[1]

So finally, at the age of eight, before I could do any more damage with my life, I had been saved.

But from what had I been saved?

I went home unsure about what had actually happened. What had I been converted into, exactly? I felt new for only a few days. And besides, I still had six more years with Stepdad from Hell, with whom sin would continue to be a full-contact sport, not to mention another twenty-five or thirty years of caustic memories I wouldn't be able to leave behind.

So what of my conversion? What of any of ours? Did anything happen when we got Jesus off the streets and into our hearts? And if so, what did it matter if nothing really changed in our lives?

———————

I have often tried to figure out the exact moment everything went to hell in my life. But there was no exact moment; my life, it seemed, was the exact moment. But over the last several years, as I have opened up about my story, I've found people who have felt the same as me. I wasn't alone.

Robert and Ann were married in 1994. We were all part of the same young married group at our church. At the time, none of us had kids, so we went to the movies together, ate out together, and got our young careers moving along together. I still got inklings about people in those days, but I dismissed my inklings about Robert because "he had a way with people." And so did I. I should have known.

"We know each other when we meet."

Robert was molested as a child, and his desire to control everything in his path from that point forward began. Mind control was his goal. Because he couldn't control the mind of the one who had violated him, it became his ambition to control the minds of those *he* violated.

From day one Robert's marriage was a ruse. He loved Ann, but his self-love was greater as he began looking for women to satisfy what was lurking in his heart. Though covered over in good looks, charm, and people skills, Robert was a broken man, and eventually there would be too many affairs to count.

I used to look down on those who had set their life's GPS just two degrees shy of hell, but after my own personal trip there, I realized our enemy punches in the coordinates for us. Yes, we might have followed every ding we heard, but we didn't know where we were headed or how to override the system.

The day always comes when the jig is up, and when it does, we will have to punch in *new* coordinates for a *new* destination if we want a *new* life. The temptation to follow the rerouting prompts is powerful, though not too powerful to ignore. And if we want a life that isn't driven by our past hurts, we must squeeze ourselves onto a tiny dirt road and trust that it will lead us somewhere good.

For Robert, the jig was up in 2007, when he finally (and fortunately) got caught. He didn't know it at the time, but he was about to be converted. Initially he thought it would be easier to ditch his marriage and run—that he wasn't worthy of redemption. And it's true that there was a short sale on Robert's life, and the balance of debts against him was greater than the total proceeds of his life. But

God was about to wreck him with love anyway—love that would come from the one he deserved the least, but who loved him the most. And her love went something like this.

"Get out!"

Ann kicked Robert out. She was done. Finished.

She pulled the chain across the door and told him it was over.

In 2001, I set out to make peace with God. By then I hadn't had a good night's sleep in a couple of years. I was worn out from the war in my chest that started on my twenty-eighth birthday. I wasn't really searching for peace at the time; I was searching for honesty. I was tired of pretending to believe that God cared, intervened, healed things up, or kept his promises.

I had been more than fair with him. I was positive and plucky. I prayed for people who needed prayer and assured them God would make a way for them. But internally I was falling apart. I pleaded with God and at times demanded an answer but heard nothing back. I might have been the worst worship leader in America between 2001 and 2007. When I wasn't drinking to kill the dead in me, I was cross-examining God to my heart's content. But on Sunday, I would sing of his mighty attributes—the very attributes that had drawn people into his snare, the ones I no longer believed were true. I sang his songs for him. I told others they could trust in him. I knew I was a liar, though no more a liar than God himself.

The opening line of the song "The Chain," by Ingrid Michaelson, tells us that the heavens are an angry place, and angry was how I imagined God felt about me. I couldn't fake it any longer; the pre-tending had become clumsy and I no longer felt at home in my own faith.

I was beyond the worry now—beyond the fear that I'd lose my soul. There were bigger fish to fry. And if *this* was life with God, all these unmatched socks tossed around in the drum of a dryer, I was no longer interested.

It was time to settle things once and for all. I needed to tell God the truth—truth that would come from the one who had told it the least, but who loved him the most. And the truth went something like this.

"Get out!"

I kicked God out of my life. I was done. Finished.

I pulled the chain across the door and told him it was over.

THE AGE OF RECKONING
Symptoms of a Deeper Problem

Our secrets have taken our past; they hold us hostage in the present. They must be outed before they destroy the rest of us.

When I was twenty-eight, I could tell you exactly how many drinks each person at the table had drunk. I knew who had left their bottles of beer, glasses of wine, or cocktails unattended and for how long. I could no longer focus on the conversations I had once been able to engage in while at dinner with friends. My mind had been hijacked by alcohol, and I never saw it coming. It consumed my thoughts, crowding out even those wonderful things such as my daughter, my wife, my work, my hopes and dreams. Alcohol is "cunning, baffling, powerful."[1] Yes. It is. I simply didn't know.

By the time I reached my twenty-eighth birthday, I had already been married for five years. Heather had just given birth to our first daughter, Chloe, and I was several years into my clergyman career. So much baggage comes with being a minister. Either you get lumped into a category with Catholic priests who've had sex with altar boys, or parishioners have unrealistic expectations of you, thinking that if *you* pray for their spouse's cancer there's a better chance it will genuflect before your prayers and scoot on out the door.

Some people believe that ministers are closer to God than they are—that we clergy types are privy to the kind of "Godformation" the rest of the world doesn't have access to. But I keep remembering how God's own Son distanced himself from the religious people of his day, mostly because their hearts were full of pride, and spent his precious time with the commoners. So good for us. We get Jesus's ear while the religious get a spiritual spanking.

I began drinking at twenty-eight. I had gotten wasted two or three times at high school parties or after football games, but I didn't know the difference between beer and vodka back then. There's a difference. I found out the hard way. The Christian college I attended, designed to prepare me for ministry, was conservative so very few people partied. When I graduated from college, I didn't drink for another six years, but when my past came crashing in on my present, I couldn't stop.

Every bad memory buzzed inside my heart like a text message I was too afraid to open. Early visits with a counselor didn't deliver the results I was looking for, and I needed something to cut the pain. For me, alcohol was that something, and it quickly became my drug of choice.

I started drinking like a normal person at first: a beer with my buddies or a glass of wine with dinner. But over the next several years, as more and more pain pushed its way into my world and cut me at the knees, the numbing part of alcohol began to kick in, and I was a goner.

The more I drank, the less I heard the penetrating voice of heartache in my soul. The alcohol was working. I no longer just wanted it but needed it, so I hid it, lied about it, thought about it all day long, and within a couple of years it consumed me.

When I was in high school, I was part of the drama club. I loved the concentration exercise we did in class. Our instructor had us lie on the floor and imagine we were in a field. "Focus on the bottoms of your feet," he'd tell us. We were supposed to feel them inside our socks first and then inside our shoes. Slowly we began to move from our toes to our legs, up to our hands, and before long I could feel the hair growing out of my head. By the end of it, we had turned our bodies inside out and were listening to our own breathing. During the fifteen minutes it took to complete the exercise, I had gotten so quiet internally that I could actually feel the blood coursing through my veins.

I felt a little exhausted when it was over. Shutting myself off from the rest of the world was hard work. But in the quiet, in the slowing down, something inside me had changed—something in the putty of who I was had been worked and bent until things had come into alignment.

As children we were once fairly malleable. As grown-ups we don't often remain that way. Yet inside of us is still the desire to have the potter's hands on us—his thumbs digging into our spirits, pushing them from here to there, keeping the putty warm so we don't turn into hardened plastic.

Every so often I come across a Bible verse I'm certain I've never read. If the passage is impactful, I wonder how I could've possibly been forty-three years old before finding it.

Jonah 2:8 says, "Those who cling to worthless idols forfeit the grace that could be theirs" (NIV 1984).

Could be. That one little phrase expects something out of me, doesn't it? It's asking for my help.

Alcoholics Anonymous often discusses character defects. When I started the program, I couldn't tell you what mine were, but the more time I spent with the brave and courageous souls who attended, watching them turn our meetings into confessionals, the more aware I became of my own defects. I had followed God for years but somehow misplaced my own statute of limitations. Others—my wife, Heather; my best friend, Brian; even my coworkers—could easily see my character defects. They all knew. But sometimes our friends let us run around with dirt on our faces and food between our teeth if they believe that our character defects are hardened plastic rather than malleable clay because they're not sure we can do anything about them anymore.

Of course I have my friends' character defects pegged. One friend lives in terrible fear of anything and everything, another is as stubborn as a mule, and another is desperate for the riches of this world. Seeing the shortcomings of others is a breeze. But seeing our own worthless idols, the things we've hidden in the folds of our everyday lives that are keeping us from the serenity that *could be* ours, is the real work of life.

Working in the church, I am stunned by the vast number of Christians forfeiting the grace that could be theirs. We have followed God for decades but can't seem to rattle off our own worthless idols because we are too busy running around with vacuum cleaners, cleaning up after ourselves so no one sees our messes.

Last week, my daughter Chloe and I went shoe shopping and saw something neither of us had seen before: high-heel tennis shoes. The top of them looked like regular tennis shoes, but the soles were three-inch heels fit for the red carpet. I'm all for trying new things, but I'm guessing they didn't make much of a splash at fashion week.

The journey toward understanding our worthless idols is much like walking onto an indoor track wearing high-heel tennis shoes. At first we will stumble and most likely roll our ankles, but if we hold out our arms for balance and take it one step at a time, eventually we'll find our rhythm and get around that track. It won't be easy at first, so we must keep at it.

Not many of us love the word *discipline*, but it is a critical prerequisite to our journey inward. Discipline expects something out of us we are not always sure we have to give. Let me save you a little trouble: you're right; you don't have it to give. If you did, discipline wouldn't be knocking on your door. It's there to pinpoint what you're lacking and then find a way, whatever it takes, to get that lacking thing inside you.

Discipline is not waiting outside the conference room at work to see you if you'd like to grab a cup of coffee after your big meeting that went south. Instead it pulls you aside and says, "Hey, what happened? Here are the things you need to do differently," and then follows up to make sure you did what you promised to do. It might not feel good, but discipline is a requirement for change.

When our home life needs recalibrating, Heather is usually the one to say, "Let's have a meeting, do some strategizing, and get everyone on the same page." But I don't want a meeting and I don't want to strategize. I want to watch TV, even though every time we have our meeting, things begin to run much more smoothly. Stuff around the house gets picked up and put back where it belongs; our dog, Mimi, gets let out when the girls come home from school; dinners are made, bills are paid, and we all seem like better versions of ourselves. I don't enjoy the meetings in which we commit to the discipline of change, but I love the change that discipline produces.

If you are already the kind of person for whom discipline is not a struggle, it could be something besides discipline that is keeping you stuck. Some of our character defects have ruined our closest relationships, ended our marriages, or left us disillusioned. We've gone to the mirror for self-reflection and have seen what life *could be* but can't seem to get there. We have read twenty-five self-help books, put their theories into practice (via discipline), and have even made some progress. But the foundational *who* we are is still wrecked, and we can't seem to shake it off. We feel we've been left with no choice but to accept the broken reality that says, "Real change is not possible for you." So we continue to manage our lives by using unhealthy coping mechanisms (worthless idols) while risking the loss of our families, ourselves, and ultimately the grace that *could be* ours. We never commit to true and lasting change because ...

We are afraid.

I know. Join the club. We all are.

Fear is very good at keeping people stuck.

We are afraid because the putty of who we are has sat around and become hardened plastic, and we're pretty sure the change we are desperate for isn't going to be pushed into alignment easily. In fact, a breaking must occur. Simply put, it's going to be painful. But the path of recovery is painful before it is peaceful. Accepting this reality will rightsize our expectations and benefit us.

Few people in life have shown us what it is to start over. Every now and then we hear a story of someone who has completely wiped the slate clean, but most often symptoms are only refereed while no significant work is completed. Still, our lack of know-how is not a free pass to remain the same, because internally we will always know the truth.

Author Susan Forward says,

> No matter how confused, self-doubting, or ambiva-
> lent we are … we can never entirely silence the inner
> voice that always tells us the truth. We may not like
> the sound of the truth, and we often let it murmur
> just outside our consciousness, not stopping long
> enough to listen. But when we pay attention to it,
> it leads us toward wisdom, health, and clarity. That
> voice is the guardian of our integrity.[2]

It seems that almost to the day I turned twenty-eight, the inner voice pushed past my subconscious and wouldn't stop chattering. When I couldn't suppress it, I started using alcohol because I didn't like what it had to say. The alcohol worked for a while but eventually began sucking good things from my life, one by one. This is when I found myself at a crossroads: continue on the same as before or listen to the inner voice that *always* tells the truth.

I didn't give myself over to recovery easily. At first I stood against it, trying to get it to compromise with me. I wanted to go through it but not surrender to it. Essentially I wanted straight teeth without braces, muscles without going to the gym, serenity without letting go of the negative coping mechanisms.

I wanted grace without forfeiting any of my worthless idols.

A good friend in recovery told me I needed to get to the root of why I was using.

"Why do you think you drink, Matt?" he asked me one night after a meeting.

"Because I like the taste."

"Do you like milkshakes?"

"Of course I do. Who doesn't?"

"When was the last time you drank ten of them? I mean, seriously, how thirsty are you?" He stood there laughing while I felt exposed. But I knew he was right. I was using.

One year from the date of that conversation, I threw myself wholeheartedly into recovery. I went to 12-Step recovery meetings, found Doug the Counselor and started back into therapy, and hung out with friends who understood recovery principles and practiced emotionally healthy living.

But I had to do the work.

The mistake of thinking that God is all you need to get this figured out is a mistake you're going to feel. That would be like walking into a grocery store hungry and thinking, *This place is all I need*, but never purchasing a thing to eat. Just because you are in a grocery store doesn't mean you get nourished. You have to shop.

So that's what I did. I shopped.

I combed the aisles looking for hope, peace, love, and self-acceptance. Sometimes I would pull out a wad of coupons to get things at clearance prices but found that you get what you pay for and full price is always best.

―――――――――――

Twenty-eight.

It was my age of reckoning—the magic number. And I see it all the time. people graduate from school and settle into a routine, launching their careers and getting married or starting a family, and merrily they roll along all the livelong day. But then something happens. The clouds roll in and within no time at all it's raining—just a drizzle at first, but within a few years, cats and dogs.

Our first go-to explanation is usually our career or boss, our spouse or partner, our lack of spirituality (or wrong spirituality), and then of course our fail-safe: the parents. But as I've always heard, you cannot solve an internal problem with an external solution, and if this is true, the problem lies smack-dab in the middle of our chests. *We* have a problem, and our only chance to remedy this problem is by going after it internally.

I did my best to transform my external world but realized I was only masking the symptoms of a much deeper problem. Something more was going on, and it was going on *within* me.

I had a core wound that needed to be addressed. But before I could address it, I would need to find it.

A stanza from T. S. Eliot's *Four Quartets* says:

> We shall not cease from exploration
> And the end of all our exploring
> Will be to arrive where we started
> And know the place for the first time.[3]

I sat in Doug the Counselor's office week after week for several years. I wasn't being realigned; I was being broken. Together we chipped away at the denial that had become a thick wall of plaster. Sometimes we made great strides, while at other times we dug at a tiny stubborn piece I thought might never come loose. But we kept at it until I began to see some of the missing pages of my story.

Finally one day, bruised and out of breath, I punched clean through the wall. Light poured in from the other side as I stepped in for a closer look. I wanted to know what had been keeping me stuck all these years. I peered through the hole, and my core wound was sitting in the ruins of my life. It was a suitcase of pain I had never unpacked.

I stepped through the hole. The debris of denial crunched under my feet as I approached the suitcase. I was cautious at first because not all of it was in the light, but as I got closer, I saw several words scrawled on the side of it.

Insecure. Unloved. Abused. Broken.

None of these words scared me, because I already knew about each of them. But another word was there—a word I wasn't expecting. I knelt down before it and traced each letter with my finger. And in the faintest whisper, loud enough for me alone to hear, I found the courage to say the word out loud, for the very first time in my life.

Incest.

PUT AWAY THE GLITTER
God Wants You to Tell the Truth

Some of the best Christians I've ever known are the
worst pretenders. Without their honesty to call a spade
a spade, we'd all be living in Pleasantville.

When God was thirteen, he never faced any kind of trial. I imagine that when he was in his twenties, he cared for himself and enjoyed the presence of his own good nature. He knew nothing of bar fights, divorce, dead children, molested girls in India, tsunamis tearing through Third World villages, violence and vigilantes, terrorists, swindlers, creeps, bad pastors, mothers leaving, fathers beating, or spouses cheating. Nor did he suffer through having extra chromosomes, issues with gender identity, cancer, blindness, missing limbs, depression, schizophrenia, or suicidal thoughts. He was free and clear. He was happy. He was content, treated well by himself, worthy, congenial, alive, and whole.

And then on the sixth day, God said, "Let us make mankind in our image" (Gen. 1:26).

You could argue that he created pain on that day—that he brought it on himself, if not on us.

God is love.

If this is true, it has to mean something different from what modern Christendom has been telling us.

We have our children put glitter on pictures of the greatest God-massacre of all time: Noah's ark. Millions of people drowned outside of the ark during the great flood. There is a hidden message beneath all the glitter we've used to cover over this mass extermination: be careful of God. Stay out of his way, do what he says, and listen to whom he calls, even if the person builds a boat and tells you it's about to rain. If you don't listen, he will drown you and your children. So good luck, and remember: God is love.

If God is love, put away the glitter, because it isn't that kind of love.

I've heard the words "Be all in for God" ever since I was a boy. They were prayed in prayer circles. They were used to twist our arms into committing more of our lives to Jesus.

"God, we want *all* of you" was a common prayer, spoken with sincere hearts. But what were we really after?

The assumption was that if we got "all of God," we would be transformed into people with no problems or, at the very least, problems picked up on sale but used only to add a little flavor to our spiritual stew. Getting all of God was much more about us than him. Our real intention was to get something for ourselves once we got all of him. We wanted our problems to go away and we wanted to be loved. That's it. But if his love isn't glitter, sooner or later we're going to realize that getting all of him is equally delicious *and* painful.

Personally speaking, I don't know any other way to live. I've tried to be the casual acquaintance of God. I've spent a fair amount of time not wanting all of him. I'm afraid of all of him because at times it feels as though God just might be the "someone" the Indigo Girls wrote about in their song "Prince of Darkness."

"Someone's got his finger on the button in some room."[1]

It's not okay. It will never be okay to see people give their all to God, to ask for all of his glory, and then watch as preventable things such as dead children and mental illness blow up in their faces, explosions that seem to have been detonated by the very hand of God.

"It wasn't him. He didn't cause it. It's because of free will!" I know how to mitigate on his behalf. But hollow reasons come hand in hand with the glitter. There's a time for glitter: parties, for instance, or preschool. But sprinkling God's story and our own with glitter is as awkward as leg warmers on a dog. It makes perfect sense when you're five. It's even cute when you're ten. But at fourteen, when you are being dragged into Grandpa's woodshed for things that will alter your spiritual and emotional chemistry forever, reasons sprinkled with glitter can make you suicidal.

I recently had a conversation with a man who believed it wasn't in the best interest of anyone to hear the lurid details of another man's painful story.

"He needs to put it in two pages," he said to me, "and keep the rest of the story focused on the redemption part. No one wants to hear all of that."

Glitter.

He was asking someone who'd been to hell and back to put a bright red ribbon on a grenade, and I knew in my heart it wasn't right.

"I want to hear it," I told him.

"Why?" he asked. "It's gratuitous, and parts of it are disgusting."

"Because parts of it *were* disgusting," I said, trying to explain. "My wife just got back from India. She was there to help establish aftercare homes for little girls in Mumbai who had been trafficked into sexual slavery. Before being rescued, many of the little girls were servicing up to fifty men every single day. Putting it in two pages would be like going on a mission into the brothels of Mumbai and after only one day saying, 'I've seen enough. The rest is gratuitous. When do we get to the redemption part?'

"If there is a God, he was there. He was in the brothels, standing in the corner of those seedy, dank rooms watching those little girls be violated over and over, not seeing the light of day for months on end. He participated in their horrors by being present. That's not gratuitous; that's the truth. And if God really is who I hope he is, I need to know that he watched. I need to know he saw it all and didn't turn away for a second. I need to know those little girls were never out of his sight—that they were never alone. That's what I need to know.

"And if we can't handle *that* about God, then we can't *handle* God at all."

When someone is burned out on drugs or alcohol, family or friends might host an intervention. During the intervention, they read letters of hope and love to their addicted friend or family member. They beg the person to stop using and say, "We want you back." They intervene.

But how does God intervene? It's clear he doesn't pull the filthy man off the terrified twelve-year-old Indian girl. He allows backpack bombs to detonate as innocent Boston bystanders have their limbs blown off on a day of celebration. Pain, it seems, is a part of who God is or, at the very least, something he uses. And it's okay for us to not be okay with this. It's not the way I would do things or, I imagine, the way you would either. So could we simply speak these words out to God? Could we say, "This isn't right … Why would you ever …?" Could we let the disappointment part our lips as we ask God to give an account of where he was the day Tutsi Rwandans were sawed in half by their own Hutu brothers? "Where were you?" we must cry out if we are ever to find an honest place with God.

But our faith has been focused on how to pray the pain away, become strong enough to overcome it, or rise above it if it has been too stubborn to leave (addiction, health issues, and so on). We have failed to give such passages as John 16:33—"In this world you will have trouble"—credence in our spiritual understanding of God and are often caught off guard when broken-down things are beyond repair.

We've been told that pain is a part of life and always will be— told by God himself to expect it—yet we do everything we can to extract any sort of darkness from our lives. In his book *Things Hidden*, Richard Rohr talks about our capacity to hold both dark and light simultaneously:

> God wants useable instruments who will carry the
> mystery, the weight of glory and the burden of sin

simultaneously, who can bear the darkness and the light, who can hold the paradox of incarnation—flesh and spirit, human and divine, joy and suffering, at the same time, just as Jesus did.[2]

Yet the core conviction of most Christians I know is this one dangerous message:

No more pain.

Pray against it, walk away from it, ignore it, hate it, or try to outlive it. But when our faith is built upon a theology of no more pain, we fail to hold dark and light together and cannot experience the fullness of God. It could even be said that we willfully reject his fullness.

Numerous spiritual books and resources about overcoming life's obstacles are available, most of which are baiting us to believe that the dangerous message of no more pain is true. Because of this, believers are in a continuous pattern of waiting for the clouds to part so they can have their lives back. They want light, and they will be satisfied with nothing less. But if we continue to make "No more pain" our mantra, we can fully expect to feel disillusioned by God—to feel that he has disappointed us terribly or abandoned us—when he's made it perfectly clear that we "will have trouble."

In this book, before you turned to the first page of chapter 1, the following scripture was printed. I wouldn't blame you if you didn't notice it. I have skimmed right past scriptures like this too. But I want you to read it now and, after you do, close your eyes and take a moment with it. Don't give the words any other meaning besides what they seem to be saying. This time take them at face value.

> I form the light *and* create darkness,
>> I bring prosperity *and* create disaster;
>> I, the LORD, do *all these things*. (Isa. 45:7)

Why do we ignore this kind of scripture? My guess is we prefer celebration to suffering, resurrection to crucifixion. We prefer there to be no more pain. Who doesn't? But faith built on preference is capable of producing only an incomplete theology; in fact, it already has.

The King James Version of that same scripture says, "I create evil."

It's not easy for us to think of God this way, but he isn't asking us to make excuses for him. I don't believe that God created injustice any more than I believe he created his own crucifixion, but he certainly allows for it, a thought that often either paralyzes or disgusts me. And we must give our paralysis, shock, and disgust a voice.

I love that Job talked *to* God and not simply *about* him. And God loved it too. When Job said, "It's not fair," he didn't say it to his friends; he said it directly to God's face. There's a difference.

In the movie *The Color Purple*, Celie has two children by the man she believes is her father. As soon as she gives birth, both times he steals her babies from her arms and gives them away. He is her greatest offender.

While leaving the room with her second child, he turns to her and says, "You better not tell nobody but God,"[3] which is exactly what she does. Celie's honest and painful communion with God becomes the hallmark of the movie. It is what keeps her sane throughout the great burden of her life.

I don't know if we have done the same. We assume God already knows, but do we ever say, "It's not fair," directly to his face? If you haven't, what kind of relationship is it, exactly?

If some of my colleagues had witnessed the exchanges I had with God while processing the grief and sadness of my past, I'm not sure what they would've taken me for—most likely not one of God's devoted followers. But in my anger, resentment, rage, and disrespect, I trusted God not to turn me out into the streets. I trusted him instead to love me, accept me, and forgive me.

Sometimes when I've said all I've needed to say, God says back to me, "I'm sorry for all you've gone through, Matthew." And then when I've accused him and spoken the kind of words that would make your blood run cold, he's simply said, "Are you finished?" This natural back-and-forth is our relationship. And in this *honest* place with him, I can feel the sharp edges of my pain softening.

Is it a risk to put God on trial? Yes. But it's a risk I'm willing to take. Do I think I have the right to question God? Do I think I have the right to be angry and express that anger? I guess the same rights a son would have.

I have found that I cannot be in deep, meaningful relationships with people if I can't be honest with them. So if people who struggled to accept me as I am needed a place to stay, I would likely set them up in the basement. They wouldn't be invited into my regular living space because then I'd have to walk on eggshells around them. And they certainly wouldn't be invited into my dining room because my dining room is reserved for friends—friends who know me and let me speak honestly, directly, and freely. Friends who accept me as I am.

I wonder if God's basement is also crowded with those of us he doesn't trust—you know, the fringy sort who pretend things are good, who never trust the relationship enough to speak up and tell him the truth. Maybe God liked Job and David best because they were honest with him. Were they afraid? Probably. But not too afraid to tell him exactly what they thought or write songs that accused him and put him on trial.

Maybe when it comes to pain, God prefers Psalms to Proverbs: sad songs to witty anecdotes, questions to solutions. Maybe he longs to hear our hearts speak out in pain, even if in the end we blame him.

I wonder if there are only a few who sit in God's dining room, not because we haven't been invited but because if we RSVP that we're coming, honesty is required. Maybe God's dining room, same as mine, is reserved for only friends—friends who accept him *as he is*, who don't pretend to be happy if they're not, who tell him the truth.

I recently asked Kara, a woman we hired to play fiddle in our church, if she would tell me about her faith journey. She swept her hair behind her ear, took a deep breath, and began like this: "Okay, I'll tell you, but I have to know that it won't get me fired." She was dead serious.

Tears filled my eyes immediately because I could hear how the body of Christ had most likely treated her. "You will never have to worry about that with me," I told her. "I just want to hear your story."

She spoke of her disappointment with God. When she was in her twenties and engaged to be married, her fiancé died suddenly. She told me that most of the things that had been communicated to her about God didn't seem true after her fiancé died and that his death sent her on a mission to gain a deeper understanding of what she really believed.

"All of the good in my life has a contrast," she told me, "and that contrast is where I learn the great life lessons. So when the contrast comes, I plop myself down in the middle of the pain, frustration, or unmet expectations and I wait on God. When he shows up, I begin working to hear his still small voice so that I will know what he is trying to teach me.

"I ask him, 'What is it that you want me to learn so that I can accomplish your will for my life?' I no longer spend my life trying to escape pain."

Kara has learned the beauty of holding dark and light together, right out in front of her face. "No more pain" is not the core conviction of her faith. She has put away the glitter. But have we?

I think God has grown weary of our drawings of rainbows, blue skies, and jagged green grass. "Let's put these away for now," I can imagine God saying as he takes our brightly colored crayons and places them high on a shelf where we can no longer get at them. "This picture of your life isn't really accurate anyway, is it?" he asks, dumping our bowl of glitter in the trash. "I'd really love to see what you could do with these." He is holding out some of the drabbest crayons we've ever seen, a fist filled with the colors of alone. "But before you put one mark on that page, I want you to tell me the truth."

He pulls up a chair right in front of us, takes our hands into his own, and looks us straight in the eyes. "Now," he says to us, "tell me what happened to you. I really want to know."

THE FAMILY WAY
The Uncensored Version of Your Story

*Our stories can deliver hope to others only if they
are able to see a bit of who we once were.*

I was born in November into a home with a father who didn't know
how to love me like I needed to be loved because he hadn't been
loved like he needed to be loved, like his parents needed to be loved,
and his grandparents before them needed to be loved.

A tiny blob of hope was squeezed into my chest the moment I
took my first breath. Part of that hope was for the good times (which
would come eventually). But most of it was there to get me through
the evil times, which would live with me until I had come of age and
then some.

I came home from the hospital dressed in tiny blue baby clothes.
Mom put me in a bedroom with two brothers and a stack of beds,
three high. We were close, the three of us—partners in crime and one
day, survivors. At least two of us would be.

My family was recast by the time I was three. There was a new man at the dinner table: a stranger at first and then a "father." But he was too much for me. He fought for the best of me. He squeezed the life out of me.

As small children, we waited for December to see if love was alive. Gifts and trinkets were laid beneath an artificial tree, promising that we meant something to someone—swearing that love *was* alive. On Christmas Eve, we'd tear through shiny paper and ribbons in hopes that whatever was in the packages would seep from the boxes and change our home. And maybe if we got it all over ourselves, it would change us too.

Junior high and high school were a blur. College was the first time I felt any sort of freedom in life. I made my own decisions. I let my heart out for the very first time. But before long, the fingerprint hollows from my stepdad's enduring grip appeared in my soul like fossilized wounds. Each time I tried to escape I was held tighter— held between the life I'd lived and the life that was coming to me.

I was standing at a precipice and a new life was there for the taking. I simply didn't know how to reach out and grab it.

The past called to me—it *wanted* me. It said that things didn't look good for someone like me. It reminded me that there wasn't much left of the tiny blob of hope—told me it could be rationed for a few more years but there would never be enough of it to last a lifetime. It whispered into my spirit that the "father" who had made us a stepfamily, who *squeezed* his way into us, would hold us as hostages forever.

My past haunted me like a ghost. It assured me that all the good things that came my way would eventually …

be.

squeezed.

out.

———————

Unless we are willing to escape into sentimentality or fantasy, often
the best we can do with catastrophes, even our own, is to find out
exactly what happened and restore some of the missing parts.

—Norman Maclean, *Young Men and Fire*

Incest.

Reading it is one thing; saying it out loud, another. It can stop
you dead in your tracks. It stopped me dead in mine.

I have no memory of the first time. It began before I can remember. Four? Five? Six? I'll never know for sure.

A monster had been brought into our home, and sex was all he
wanted from us. The sexual fuse he lit within us spread like wildfire
and burned our lives to the ground. He was supposed to have been
there for us, showing us the ropes of boyhood, of manhood. But
instead he abused us, and then he taught us how to abuse each
other.

My brother Tim was Stepdad from Hell's sexual apprentice.
What he did to Tim, Tim began doing to me, and before long the
entirety of our home was a full-blown brothel.

By the time I was six or seven, sexual activity with my older
brother was becoming a daily occurrence. We were close in age,
twenty months apart, so outside of our sexual relationship, we were

normal boys who played football in the backyard and fought over girls at school. But behind closed doors, the light in our spirits was so dim we could barely find our way.

Desiring my own sibling sexually wrecked me as a teenager. I never reached out for him in all our time together, but I longed for him to reach out for me. I longed for it and then was repulsed by it. But because no one knew, I mostly just longed for it.

"Want to go down to the basement?" he would ask, but I knew what he really meant.

"Sure," I'd tell him because I liked going to the basement. I wanted to go. For years I had mentioned the incest to counselors, pretending I didn't like it. But secretly I always had.

For years I carried around the shame of believing I had been complicit in our wreck of a sex life—of believing I had brought it on myself simply because I *desired* our getaways to the basement. But like so many others who have been down this road before me, the body betrays. Our bodies respond biologically to abuse, even if our hearts want nothing to do with it. And although my body's broken-down yet natural response meant nothing about who I was, before the age of reason, it meant everything.

When I was fourteen, my mom divorced Stepdad from Hell, and all sexual activity came to a halt. But the damage had already been done. The residual of that kind of power was a compounding interest that had gained enough leverage to last a lifetime, and I would spend years trying to outthink same-sex attraction.

In junior high I dreaded the locker room because I suspected that the *real* boys somehow knew they were showering with a fraud. A liar. A broken boy.

I had no business pretending to be normal. I was damaged goods. The shame was paralytic.

In high school I did my best to blend in, to pretend things were okay. But every night, shame threw me in the clink and ran a billy club across the iron bars of my cage so I couldn't sleep. It never let me forget who I really was.

By the time I reached college, I was a dead man walking. I reached out to God, but it seemed he only addressed the symptoms of my problem when what I needed was to be gutted and rebuilt. I was lost. I was not enough. I was too much. I was broken. I was not a man. And I carried the heft of this burden right into my marriage.

But Heather had been warned: "What is his family background? Just be careful."

Heather is a linear thinker, a cause-and-effect kind of girl, so it isn't in her nature to believe for the best, especially when the statistics tell another story. But for whatever reason, she had immense faith in me. She always has.

Early in our marriage I felt the weight lighten a little. I was beginning again. This was my new family, my new life. But my secrets were in a state of hibernation, and within a few years they woke from their slumber and began making accusations I couldn't defend.

Mentors, pastors, and friends told me to let it go.

"God isn't interested in your past; he's interested in your future." But I never believed them. God's own story was full of disorder, his past every bit as messed up as mine. And when God saw how out of control things had gotten, he sent his Son to clean things up. If God's past mattered that much to him, I figured mine mattered too.

I needed to see someone. I needed a therapist. That's when I found Doug.

I started slow, telling a lot of half-truths, pretending I was further along the road of recovery than I actually was. Here's the thing about therapy: you can make the story up however you want, but the truth will not bend itself around a lie.

A good therapist might let you get away with a safer version of the story for a while only because they realize your healing is a journey and not a destination. But if you are ever going to start feeling better, at some point you need to wrap yourself up in a blanket of truth and stay put until your fever breaks.

I was on and off with my therapy but continued to plod along slowly. I used close friends as a sounding board and read books about sexual abuse to gain a deeper understanding of what had happened to me. As I stepped further into the truth, I struggled to manage the negative and painful emotions. It was much easier to be drunk, so my drinking escalated out of control, which slowed my progress considerably.

But then I began working the twelve steps, which threw my recovery into overdrive.

Truth: It's painful before it's peaceful.

Count on it.

Sifting through the physical, sexual, and emotional abuse in a healthy way brought me to the end of myself, which was not a bad thing. But somewhere along the way, my eyes were opened and in time I came to understand just how sharply the distorted sexual relationship with my brother defined and categorized my brokenness.

This one broken relationship had indoctrinated me into the family way, and now I would need to find a way out that wouldn't get me fit for concrete sneakers and thrown off the Brooklyn Bridge.

I was emotionally open for business. I was hard at work, looking more deeply into my family of origin than ever, dissecting and then analyzing every microbe of my past life. And as I did, a turning began to occur. Memories that hadn't been given the time of day began transforming themselves into the truth right before my eyes.

"It was my night to stand up for dinner."

"What do you mean your 'night to stand up for dinner'?"

"I mean we had only four chairs but there were six of us, so two of us had to stand," I explained. "So because I was standing, I had easy access to the pot of mashed potatoes sitting on the table."

"Wait, I'm confused," Heather said, putting her hand up to stop me.

"Just let me finish, Heath—this is a *good* story," I assured her, and it was. The mashed potato fight had gone down in history, and I couldn't believe that after eight years of marriage I hadn't told her about it.

"So by the time we were done, there were instant potatoes hanging off the walls like we had hired in drywall contractors. The potatoes were everywhere," I said, feeling really normal.

"Right, but I'm confused about the standing. Why were you standing up for dinner? Did you always stand up for dinner?" she asked like a social worker.

"Because there were *six* of us!" I was beginning to get agitated. "But there were only *four* chairs. Do the math."

"Only it's not math," she said. "It's family. And didn't you once tell me you had a formal dining room table with eight chairs that never got used? Why didn't you use those?"

"Because they were the good chairs."

She made a face. She didn't understand, so I clarified.

"The fabric on those chairs was very expensive," I explained.

"So you're saying you were a family of six but only had four usable chairs at the dinner table?" I was resistant. All I had wanted out of this was a good memory. "That is so sad to me, Matt." She gently reached her hand out to mine.

"It is not sad!" I said, snatching my hand away. "You are turning this into something stupid!"

"How old were you?" she asked, ignoring my outburst. There was love in her eyes, but I couldn't let it in.

"Don't do this, Heather. It's fine. I didn't mind standing up for dinner."

"How do you know? You had nothing to compare it to. I mean, if there *had* been a chair, I bet you would've sat in it."

I could feel the squeeze. This time I was being squeezed into a painful memory.

"I'm so sorry, honey," she said, scooting closer. There were tears in her eyes.

"Who even cares? Seriously." I stared at the wall, feeling terminal.

"I care," she said, reaching for me again.

I sat quietly as Heather rubbed her hand up and down my arm. I replayed the scene over in my head and could see myself standing at the edge of my childhood dinner table. Until that day, I had never questioned why we stood up for dinner. It seemed that even the good times had an undercurrent.

God, were we ever a real family?

In ninth grade the landscape of our family dramatically changed. My mom divorced our stepdad, my sister got married, my stepbrother went to live with his real parents, and Tim moved to Richmond, Virginia, to live with our biological father.

For a couple of years it was just me and Mom, and both of our lives let out a great sigh of relief. But our reprieve was fleeting because within two years my mom got married again and Tim moved back home.

From the beginning, Tim and my new stepdad didn't get along, which was no surprise. Tim didn't get along with most people. Inflicting pain onto others was his cocktail for managing the pain of his past. I know that now. So while they would argue, Mom and I would watch, and as the relationship between them spiraled, their verbal conflicts eventually became violent.

But I was tired from all the fighting I had already been through in my life. I was done. So one day in the spring of 1988, I called my biological father, packed a suitcase, bought a one-way bus ticket to Virginia, and left without saying a word.

Boarding the Greyhound bus that day was the first time I'd ever been on my own. I sat in the plush velvety seat and stared out the window, waiting for the bus to take me to a life that wouldn't include

Tim and his chaos, Stepdad from Hell, my new stepdad, my sister, my mom, the lies, the brokenness, the shame—any of it. I couldn't wait to see the road stretch out before me. I could already hear it singing, "Here come better days."

Somehow my mom had caught wind that I was leaving, and just as the bus was pulling out of the station, she careened into the parking lot on two wheels. She jumped from her two-toned Chevy Citation and scanned the large tinted windows, desperate to find me. We had become so close during our two years together, but in order to find my own way, I had to give her up. I hoped one day she'd understand.

With tears streaming down her cheeks and a hand over her mouth to stifle the cries, she stood waving me on to my father. I didn't expect my heart to be broken—after all, I was getting out. But the expression on her face grieved me so deeply that I could barely breathe. One look at her face and I knew her heart was broken too. It had been too much—for both of us.

I was in Richmond for less than two days before I headed back to Ohio. My dad told me I could stay, but like a teenager I already missed my friends and decided to go home.

You would have thought we were driving from Richmond to Greenland. The return trip was a total of twenty-six hours, and the bus was filled to capacity most of the way home.

I was stuck in the middle of the very back seat. On one side of me was a hulking man wearing sunglasses and a leather cap. At one point I think he stared out the window for twelve straight hours. On the other side of me was a smallish, thin man with dirty jeans and body odor. He and I were jammed together because Big Leather Cap took up more than his fair share of space, squeezing the two of us into what was left.

In *Jesus, My Father, the CIA, and Me*, writer Ian Morgan Cron speaks about the wounding of those who do not know the love of their father, and how they "begin life without a center of gravity." He goes on to say, "Many of us who live without these gifts that only a father can bestow go through life banging from guardrail to guardrail.... We know each other when we meet."[1]

I was a runaway that day, and I'm pretty sure the man with dirty jeans and body odor was too and that both of us were banging from guardrail to guardrail. I couldn't have been sure, as I was only seventeen at the time and understood so little about the underbelly of life, but there was something in his eyes and I suppose something in mine.

We know each other when we meet.

I didn't know his backstory, but I didn't have to. It's like meeting second cousins at a family reunion. You look at them and instantly recognize their high cheekbones just like yours, or their deep-set eyes just like yours, or their pain—just like yours. This man's pain was no different than mine. And a runaway knows a runaway, every time.

There will always be those of us whose lives seem to have been written from something like Becky's pen, each harsh and chaotic word marking up our souls for good. And this kind of pain is somewhat different from the pain of those who have been traditionally redeemed. It doesn't happen all at once but rather is ongoing in our lives, causing us to wince when we least expect it. But it can also remind us of our need for something else, for some*one* else, or maybe just keep our hearts softened for when we stumble upon another runaway.

For then we could be useful.

I have heard it said that God wastes nothing—that every bit of our pain will one day be useful. Dan Allender, a renowned author and counselor, says, "It is out of our wounds, from the core ache within us, that we find our calling."[2]

I believe this is true. Because once I stopped banging from guardrail to guardrail, I realized I was on the same road I had always been on—the same road I'd always *be* on. I just needed to get in the right lane.

And now as I continue down this road, telling others how a runaway like me with a backstory like mine is finding his way, I am also finding friends—or maybe they are finding me.

PART 2

COMPATHY

AND WEE DANCED
The Hope of God

*Friends of mine have a beautiful Goldendoodle named Hopey
Grace. She jumps on them the second they get home from work.
"No, Hope. That's enough, Hope," they say. But Hope presses
forward anyway, with great enthusiasm. If she's asleep on the floor,
they'll call her over—"Come here, Hope. Come sit next to me."
I've watched them take her muzzle in their hands and tell her,
"Hopey Grace, you are just so precious." She can be a lot to handle.
And she's definitely more than they bargained for. But Hope is a
permanent fixture in their lives. She isn't going anywhere soon.*

"It's stage-four metastatic adenocarcinoma breast cancer," she told
me over the phone. "They think it's in my lungs, liver, uterus, and
ovaries."

"How sure are they?"

"They are running several tests to make sure, but they are fairly
certain."

Just ten days earlier my sister, Trina, had updated her Facebook status with a message that read, "Five years today I am cancer-free. Thank you, God! It's time to celebrate life!" A tiny red heart and smiley face punctuated the message, which has always been her style: happy.

Over the next few weeks, we came to understand that although not in her ovaries, the cancer had spread to her spleen and bones and there was a spot in her brain.

To say this news was overwhelming is an understatement. Trina is the rest of us; she's all that's left. Tim died in 1992, and I assumed that the odds of death by tragedy were in my favor. One person dying young per family unit is more than enough, and I was certain God would agree.

It simply wasn't fair, especially because the dust had only just begun to settle in Trina's life.

She was barely nineteen when she got up the nerve to make a run for it. We had grown up in a war zone, doing our best to survive the sexual predator in our home, and then one day Trina took off and married the man of her dreams.

But love is tricky.

When you've experienced only abuse from the man who claims to be your father figure, love gets dug up and formed from the clay of "unabuse" rather than true love. The abused have expectations on a whole different level than those who have experienced authentic and unconditional love. The abused are likely to see a person who holsters their fists as their one true love simply because that person isn't prone to violence. And so for Trina, a troubled childhood was fodder for a troubled marriage.

I was in sixth grade when she left home. I saw a half-packed suitcase open on her bed and realized this was it—this was her swan song. I ran into my room to find a sheet of notebook paper. I wrote her a letter and hid it in her suitcase. If I could've stowed away in the elastic sock bin of that suitcase, I would have. I would've disappeared with her forever, and we would've listened to Barry Manilow, Joan Jett, and Don Henley for the rest of our lives. But she couldn't take me with her, so I had to let her go.

Thirty years later, the idea of letting her go again, this time for good, is appalling.

The day the test results were due back, I spent the afternoon driving. I had a counseling appointment but left the house early because I couldn't sit around waiting any longer. As I wandered the streets of my college alma mater, rather than worry alone, I called Trina.

"When do you get the results?"

"It's supposed to be at one or one thirty."

"Why don't you call them now? If they're in at one, I'm guessing they'll be in at eleven."

"Because I'm not really in a hurry to find out," she told me.

I understood. "Is Chuck with you?" Chuck was her big, new, beautiful boyfriend. He had quickly become her rock.

"You know he is," she told me, smiling through the phone.

Still unsettled, I got off the phone, parked the car, and paced a city block to get rid of the nervous energy. The sign out front of an old church in Anderson, Indiana, read, "A Place for Everyone." Walking around the building, I pulled on five or six door handles, looking for a way in. Apparently it wasn't a place for everyone. I had given my life's work to the church but couldn't get inside this one to pray that my sister's cancer results would be negative.

After thoroughly casing the joint, I came across another door with a message that read, "Press the Doorbell for Assistance." There was a broken-down doorbell I was sure had been picked up at the local junkyard. It didn't budge beneath the weight of my finger, but a skeptical voice hissed at me anyway.

"Hello?" It was the voice of an unhappy woman. She wasn't having any of it.

"I'd like to come in and pray," I said back. There was a quick buzzing sound, and I pulled on the handle.

When I entered the church, I considered checking in to show that I wasn't a vagrant or swindler but instead nosed my way around, sniffing for the sanctuary.

I walked into the sanctuary and God was already there. At times he is as quiet as an introvert, and when I hear that kind of silence, I know he's watching me. For only a second I thought about sitting in the front row, but I didn't like the commitment of it so I opted for the second. I stared at the platform where on weekends the pastor spoke to the attendees about God, told them there was hope, told them Jesus died to set them free from whatever baggage had followed them into church that day.

The room was stunning. It had been beautifully preserved for at least a hundred years. A stained-glass window hanging over the baptistry caught my eye. There was an image in the glass with something written beneath it. Two men were fashioned from the glass: one was Jesus, but the other, I wasn't sure. Peter? Judas? I moved in for a closer look.

It was John the Baptist. The two of them were standing in the Jordan River with a dove flying over their heads. It was a good story. Someone had baptized God. I had never understood the story, but people seemed to like it.

The sign below it read, "Suffer it now for thus it becometh us to fulfill all righteousness."

I'm sure that in my state of despondency it was supposed to mean something powerful to me, but the only word I saw was *suffer*. *But why?* I thought. *Why suffer?*

When I turned around, the beauty of the church nearly took my breath away. I had grown up in a small-town church made mostly of cinder blocks. It was the place where my uncle told us that Debby Boone was a no-good hussy for singing secular songs like "You Light Up My Life." This was not that church.

The walls were covered in stained glass, letting filtered light into the darkened corners of the room while softening old plaster walls. I could feel the presence of their liturgy, hundreds of God's promises rolling off the tongues of those who had gathered in this space week after week, year after year, decade after decade. They probably sat in the pews and wondered at the things of God, yet for all their wondering, things hadn't come any clearer. Because in the end, we all suffer—some more than others, a random roll of celestial dice, it seems.

I made my way through the room, finding a back hallway with stairs that led to a beautiful mezzanine. The regality of this sanctuary stood in such stark contrast to the run-down love in my heart. My now-quiet God had been kept away in this cold and beautiful room when he could have been hard at work healing lepers and setting people free.

I walked the rows of the mezzanine, which formed a U shape over the top of the sanctuary. If this were my church, this is where I would be sitting. I imagined it was where they kept the bandits, hookers, thieves, and drug addicts, along with those who suffered for no good reason.

I sat in the back row this time and stared out at the vacant church. I didn't wait for God to start a conversation with me. I didn't wait for him to tell me why my sister had cancer.

"Go ahead and heal her," I told him. I wanted to know that after all she had been through, there would be more to her life than a painful death in the clutch of cancer. "She needs more time to be loved the right way, more time to find out who she really is apart from the brokenness. She deserves to be happy. She deserves life, not death. She deserves to be redeemed."

I might as well have been staring down the barrel of a gun, saying, "Go ahead and shoot me." He might and he might not. Either way it didn't matter. I already had sorrow's theme song memorized. I could sing it in my sleep.

As soon as I left the church, my phone rang. "The test results won't be back until next week," she told me. "They said it would probably be Tuesday."

"Probably? That is ridiculous! Why is it taking so long?"

"They said biopsies take a while. Apparently the specimen has to sit for a couple of days before it tells them what they need to know. I don't really understand it. So we're just waiting and praying."

"Okay," I said with a little more grace. "And I'm guessing you're probably okay with that."

"Totally. Chuck and I are going on a motorcycle ride tonight and I'm gonna enjoy myself." I smiled at how she could always manage to find a way out of her unhappiness. And I loved Big New Beautiful Boyfriend. He was one of the sweetest people I had ever met.

But then she spoke words that went straight through me. Maybe they shouldn't have, but they did.

"They anointed me at church yesterday—for healing."

"Good," I said right away. "I'm happy, Trina." But I wasn't happy at all.

———

Healing confused me as a child. It was something I was supposed to believe in, but it all seemed like one big crapshoot. Once in a while someone got their healing while the rest died. And most of the ones who said they'd been healed died anyway. "They finally got their *ultimate* healing," their loved ones would say, meaning they were in heaven. I realize that this sort of thing makes some people feel better, but it makes others feel they've been conned.

C. S. Lewis said, "I pray because I can't help myself. I pray because I'm helpless. I pray because the need flows out of me all the time, waking and sleeping. It doesn't change God, it changes me."[1] I wonder if he said this before his wife died or after. If he said it before, I'd know he wrote a good sermon that inspired people to believe he was a man of deep thought. If he said it after, those same people would believe he was a man of deep faith. If he said it before she died, they'd believe *in* him. If he said it after, they'd just believe him.

Maybe the most faithful prayer isn't "Change me, God" but "God, change."

If my sister dies, I'll ask him to change me then but not today. Not yet. Today I'm still praying that God will change himself—that he'll recognize the error of his ways, baptize himself, and start over. That he'll say, "What have I done?" and cure her instantly. If he did, I'd forgive him for all the rest: for the war zone of a childhood, for allowing a sexual predator into our home, for what happened between my brother and me. If he saved my sister, I swear I'd wipe the slate clean between us. I'd fix up my run-down love, renovate the slums of my heart, and start over with him.

That afternoon I spent the better part of my counseling session informing my counselor, Doug, about Trina's health and imploring that he clarify why life is so random and chaotic with God at the helm.

"Why is this happening now?" he said, repeating my question. "When your sister is finally getting out from under all the pain in her life—when she finally has a chance at peace?" He paused and stared out his window, looking for an answer. "Matt, I wish I knew."

Then his eyes narrowed and he shook his head at how wrong it all seemed—at how unnecessary and tragic. It bothered him too and I was glad I had company.

We headed down the hallway to the receptionist's area. He didn't say another word, but I could feel his empathy every step of the way.

I headed out the door and saw an elderly woman standing toward the back of her car with the trunk open. Linville Services was not only a counseling center but also a safe home for battered women. This elderly woman was doing her best to lift two garbage bags filled with clothing out of her trunk. She plopped them on the ground and began dragging them up the sidewalk.

"Can I help you with those?" I asked, but she uncomfortably declined, more encumbered by my presence than by the weight of the bags, which were stretched to capacity.

"No, thank you. I'll be fine," she told me, so I left her alone.

From my car I watched her struggle to get them up the walkway. And then on my ride home I wished I'd taken the bags from her—butted right into her business and shared the load. Why hadn't she let me help? Maybe she thought, *Unless you can cure domestic violence, I don't need your help*. But we all need each other's help, even if we can't cure one another.

And I needed God's help, even if he wouldn't cure my sister.

When Tim was two years old, he couldn't say Trina's name correctly. He called her "Weena," which eventually became "Wee Wee." Sometimes her kids, who are grown and have families of their own, opt for "Wee Wee" over "Mom."

Over the years, Wee Wee was shortened to just Wee, which is how her name appears in the contacts list of my phone. To me, that's who she is.

The night after my counseling appointment, I was burdened by the day, so I cozied up in my chair, opened my laptop, and checked out of real life for a while. I received a notification on Facebook that I had been tagged in a picture. I clicked the notification, and a black-and-white photo appeared. It was a picture I hadn't seen before. It was us: me and Wee at my niece's wedding.

She looked so alive—so healthy and beautiful—and was dancing for all she was worth. We both were. At the reception, we had taken the dance floor by storm before others worked up the nerve to join in. And eventually, when the champagne had run its course, they did just that.

When I look closely at that picture, I can see us at every age. And I can see us free. Free from the pain of our childhood. Free to be what we were always meant to be.

> *Ruin pushes rubble in the city of sin, but I*
> *found love at the end of the world.*
>
> —John Mark McMillan, "Love at the End"

The world had beaten us down in our youth. It had lied to us as adults, telling us all the things we could never be. In the aftermath, we were left to push around the rubble of our brokenness—to wonder where in the world we belonged.

But the dance floor was where we thumbed our noses at life— where we salvaged a portion of ourselves because our hearts had been hidden away for far too long. It was a place we most definitely belonged—to each other.

We celebrated that night. We sweat like hogs in dress clothes. But more than that, we hoped for her daughter and son-in-law. We hoped their love would stand the test of time—that they would never give up. It's what hope does. It looks toward a bright future because it can actually feel the healing, love, and redemption crammed into its pockets.

Hope is creative and so resourceful. It can take thumbtacks and tape and stick things back together if we'll let it. Because hope survives, and so had we.

And Wee danced.

Therapists would do well to install dance floors in their offices. That way, whenever a patient was stuck, they could put on a little Usher, crank up the volume, and let them gut it out right there on the dance floor.

We kept right on dancing that night until the floor was cleared and the tables were taken down. And when the DJ finally realized the two of us weren't going anywhere, he tore down his rig and headed for home.

But there will always be another dance somewhere. And together we'll find it. And we'll dance. You can count on it.

8

LOVE SIFTING
The Comfort of God

*Isn't it obvious that God deliberately chose men
and women that the culture overlooks and exploits
and abuses, chose these "nobodies" to expose
the hollow pretensions of the "somebodies"?*
—1 Corinthians 1:27 THE MESSAGE

We measure pain and love from the day we are born. At times it feels the sands of pain are sifted so much heavier than the sands of love, and we forever wonder if it's because of something we've missed along the way or something we've done wrong. For many of us, it seems there is no such thing as grace. Most of us accept grace only after we have exhausted our options and realized that we will never be able to pay what we owe—and we are right. But grace is life, and it's all around us for the taking.

This is Ellen.

Ellen has Down syndrome. She is forty years old and loves her "gummies." Her dad, John, often takes her to the store to purchase Gummi Worms, Gummi Bears, Dots, and Orange Slices, even though her purse is already filled with them.

Three nights ago, the girls and I rode our bikes to Ellen's house, which is only a mile or so away. Ellen had a head cold and pointed to her nose several times, saying, "This hurts," showing us the wear and tear the tissue had taken on her sweet little nose.

"You're fine, Hot Dog," John kept telling her, and she would settle back down for a few minutes before telling us again how bad it hurt.

Sometimes when I'm with Ellen, I put my forehead against hers and we stare into each other's eyes. I don't know all that's behind them, but we look at each other anyway, and I feel something in my spirit that sifts the sands of love a little more evenly.

"What's your favorite pie?" she asks me.

"Cherry," I tell her. "What's yours?"

"Key lime. What's your favorite movie?"

"*Hairspray*," I say, beating her to the punch. "What's yours?"

She pauses for a moment. "*Hairspray*," she says and smiles. We've had this conversation many times, and this is when I want to eat her face. That smile. I can hardly stand how cute she is.

"Do you like *Beetlejuice*?" I ask. It's a trick question because I already know she hates *Beetlejuice*, but I like to watch her roll her eyes at how ridiculous she thinks he is.

"Do you like pancakes?" she asks, and I tell her I do. "What's your favorite kind?" she continues.

"My favorite kind of pancakes?" I ask, thinking this is where her special needs have created a gap between us. "There's only one kind of pancake that I'm aware of, Ellen." She nods her head and waits for me to answer her. "I guess I don't really know. What's your favorite kind?"

"With syrup."

"Of course. With syrup. I should have known."

This is our conversation, and it could easily go on this way for a couple of hours. Even though she asks the same questions over and over again, it's not bothersome at all and it doesn't make me uncomfortable. The sand just keeps sifting.

Last year our family spent some time in Hilton Head, South Carolina, with Ellen and her parents. One evening all of us ended up dancing to Shania Twain in the middle of the living room. Ellen had a few dance moves that were all her own and I still watch them on my iPhone when I'm feeling a little blue. At one point she threw her arms in the air and yelled out at the top of her lungs.

Whatever joy was inside her wasn't containable in that moment. Her guttural yell would have chased the dark out of any room.

At the end of the evening, after Ellen and I had gone through her list of favorite TV shows (and after she told me I looked like Cockroach from *The Cosby Show*), her mother, Betsy, came downstairs with Ellen's pajamas.

"It's time for bed, Ellen," she called over the stairs on her way down. I stared at the pajamas slung over Betsy's shoulder. I hadn't dressed my girls in their pajamas for at least seven or eight years and probably never would again. As Betsy continued mingling with her guests, I wondered about the commitment it had taken to raise Ellen. I wondered how it must have felt the first time she realized that raising Ellen would never be done. Betsy has been mothering, worrying about, and taking care of Ellen for a lifetime. It must be hard and wonderful work. Sand so evenly sifted—the pain and the love balancing each other out in the life of her extraordinary daughter.

Author Robert Farrar Capon says,

> If God seems to be in no hurry to make the problem of evil go away, maybe we shouldn't be, either. Maybe our compulsion to wash God's hands for him is a service he doesn't appreciate. Maybe—all theodicies and nearly all theologians to the contrary—*evil is where we meet God.* Maybe he isn't bothered by showing up dirty for his dates with creation. Maybe—just maybe—if we ever solved the problem, we'd have talked ourselves out of a lover.[1]

Sometimes the comfort of God comes to us dirty, showing up where we least expect it. I have often found God mixed into what many consider their greatest disappointments in life. But if we are not careful to pay closer attention, we just might miss the very thing our redemption so desperately needs.

———————

Heather and I gathered the girls into the bonus room of our home. I didn't want them to hear about Aunt Wee Wee's cancer in a place where so many of the trivial moments of their lives had played out, such as the kitchen or their bedroom. I wanted it to be set apart, sanctified, because I expected that God would be at work in that moment. And when they looked back, I hoped they would sense how he was present in the room with them, comforting them in their sadness. Maybe the location didn't matter, but to me it did. I needed to feel as though I were doing something, anything, even if it made no difference whatsoever.

"We have some bad news, girls." Chloe's face looked as if we might be getting divorced, so I got right into it. "Remember Aunt Wee Wee's breast cancer? It has come back, but worse this time. It has metastasized, which means it has spread to several places in her body." They sat quiet. I think that at fourteen and twelve years old, they didn't know how to respond. They were close to Aunt Wee Wee, so behind their vacant eyes, their hearts likely were shifting things around so this terrible news could fit on a shelf somewhere inside them.

I continued. "The doctors are saying that people who have what Aunt Wee Wee has usually live between two and four years, although some live as long as ten years. She is going to be starting chemotherapy treatments next week, and we're hoping it will have a strong effect on the cancer."

"Can the chemo kill all the cancer?" Evalee asked. I could hear the real question just below the surface.

"No, honey. The doctors are saying that her cancer is not curable."

"Why?" she asks. "What is the chemo for, then?"

"The chemo can shrink the cancer," Heather says, in full teacher mode, because she knows what Ev needs: information. "But it can't completely eliminate it because there is too much of it in her organs. It will work for a time, but not forever."

Both girls stare. There are tears in Chloe's eyes. She doesn't say a word. Heather moves in close and pulls Chloe onto her lap. "What are you thinking, Chloe?"

After staring off into space, she finally says, "I don't know what to think, Mom."

"I know, honey. Your dad and I have been processing this news for the past couple of weeks. We didn't tell you guys because we didn't have all the information." Heather did her best to keep Chloe on her lap, but Chloe's long limbs overflowed her. I followed Heather's lead and moved in next to Evalee, pulling her onto my lap.

Chloe is like me in every way. Looks like me. Wakes up happy and raring to go like me. Looks on the bright side like me. And Evalee—just like her mother. Weighs all the information before making a decision. Cautious of people she hasn't known very long, only considering them friends once they have earned it. Evidence informs her feelings, not blind love. So sitting in that room with little Heather on my lap and little Matt on Heather's lap made perfect sense. Heather could comfort Chloe because she knew how to comfort me, and I could comfort Evalee because I knew how to comfort Heather.

But empathy doesn't always play by the rules.

Before any of us said another word, I could feel Evalee's tears on my neck. I watched them drip, making dark gray circles on my light gray shirt. "You okay?" I asked her.

"Yes, Dad. I'm just worried about you. She's your sister. How are you doing? I'm sad for you, Dad."

I don't know that I should have sucked up my tears, but I did. It wasn't her job to comfort me. I still needed to be her dad. "I'm sad, Evalee, but I will be okay." And then she did something I'll never forget. She scooted off my lap and pulled both my legs onto her own. My body stiffened as she lifted my head, pulled me into her chest, and began rubbing my back. She spoke to me from a soul that all at once seemed to know something about great loss.

"I'm so sorry, Dad, but it's going to be okay." I could feel her little body beneath mine, doing its best to rock me back and forth in her arms just as I had rocked her when she was a baby—before she knew anything about cancer or death.

She was only twelve. And I was in my forties. It made no sense, but it made all the sense in the world. Even so, my body was frozen tight. I couldn't seem to let the healing wash over me.

Several weeks later, Evalee was invited to an end-of-the-year swim party with some kids from her school. Two days before the party she spent the evening bugging Heather and me about getting a new swimsuit. I finally caved.

"All right, all right. Let's just go get it now," I told her.

Evalee is more of a sporty girl, so we headed to Dick's Sporting Goods to find something that wasn't girly or trimmed with ball fringe.

After we arrived, she grabbed the first two suits she saw (she doesn't love to shop), popped into the dressing room, and in a matter of seconds popped back out wearing suit number one. It was cute on her. I could tell she liked it.

"This top is not quite right with these things," she said, pushing the pads in the bra around. "Could we check for another size?"

"Yep, I'll check. You put on the other one." After scanning for other tops and not finding any, I reported back to the dressing room area. "There are no other sizes, Ev. That was the only one."

"Who cares," she said, "'cause look at *this*!" and she sprang from the dressing room with a giant grin on her face. She had found it. It was a neon salmon top with black bottoms and it fit her perfectly.

"That's the one," I confirmed. "Love it." She smiled and came over to hug me. After a couple of seconds, she pulled away but held on to my shoulders, making deep eye contact with me. Her face was a little troubled but full of love.

"What?" I finally said.

"I'm sorry, Dad."

"About what?" I asked, thinking she felt guilty for badgering me to get her a new swimsuit. But that wasn't it.

"I'm just sorry about all of this—about what you're going through." She continued looking into my eyes. "About Aunt Wee Wee."

I stood in the middle of the women's swimsuit aisle at Dick's, held by Evalee's twelve-year-old all-knowing gaze. Only this time, instead of running, my body caved in on her little frame and I felt love sifting within me, doing what it could to balance the pain.

She had disrupted the moment with compassion and empathy—with compathy.

Her little sixth-grade hand rubbed up and down my back. I was one lucky dad.

After purchasing the swimsuit from a man who looked exactly like Captain Stubing from *The Love Boat*, we were off to get ice cream.

It was the best time I'd had in a while. It was a reprieve I hadn't known I needed. I went home with a full love tank. God had shown up dirty (my sister still had cancer), but Trina was out riding motorcycles with Big New Beautiful Boyfriend.

I don't know why some of us are dealt the hand we are dealt. I don't know why Ellen was born with Down syndrome. I don't know why my family's soul was mutilated beyond recognition in our childhood or why we would have to try so desperately hard to find ourselves again. I don't understand starvation. And I don't understand being orphaned. Sometimes it all feels like one big ill-fated mishap. But then I sit with Ellen, and for an hour or two it all makes sense, or if it doesn't, I don't seem to mind at all.

I've often heard that a burden shared is divided by two. But there are moments, in the company of those who care, when it feels as if a huge minus sign has replaced the division sign and our burdens aren't being divided at all; they're being subtracted. And subtraction is always better than division because when things are subtracted, they disappear altogether.

The people who truly love us are great at subtraction.

———————

"What are you doing on Tuesday?" Ellen asks me, rolling her index finger in a circle to get the words going.

"I'm working, Ellen. What are you doing?"

"Getting some gummies."

"Can I have another one of those Orange Slices?" I ask, even though she has already given me one.

"Yeeeees," she says, smiling. She reaches into her fuchsia sequined purse, and her little fingers rummage inside. She pulls out an Orange Slice and then gets a very serious look on her face. "Only half," she tells me.

"Only half," I say back, respecting her boundaries, even though I really want five.

I watch her focus on the Orange Slice as she meticulously rips it into two equal pieces. I hold out my hand, waiting for my half. But to Ellen, half an Orange Slice simply means ripping it in two.

"There's your half," she says with the sweetest smile, and I look down into my hand. Ellen has given me both pieces.

And love is sifting.

ME TOO
You Are Not Alone

People are screwed up in this world. I'd rather be with
someone screwed up and open about it than somebody
perfect and ... you know ... ready to explode.
—Ned Vizzini, *It's Kind of a Funny Story*

The word *saved* was the most important word of all in my church of origin. If someone had finally given in to the screaming preacher and prayed the sinner's prayer—something like, "God's good. I'm bad. Stop it!"—then that person had just switched his or her reservations in eternity. But the spiritual peer pressure came at us from many angles: Sunday school teachers, youth leaders, even the special guest singers who came in from out of town like rock stars, preaching hellfire at the end of their concerts.

The dominating message was that God wanted me to say yes no matter what and that the more difficult questions of life were unnecessary.

In children's church, I grabbed handfuls of candy from a pillowcase; I only needed to answer questions with "God" or "Jesus" or "the Holy Bible" to fill my claw with Sour Balls. And at the end of the movie by flannelgraph, my teacher would nearly insist that we "give our hearts and lives to the Lord." Daniel needed God so lions wouldn't eat him, Noah needed God to save his family from drowning, David needed God to kill a giant, and Mary needed God so she could have baby Jesus. It was simple: they needed him and so did we.

I didn't question it then, but in time it would seem as though we'd all been given free tickets to The Greatest Show on Earth, and then when we arrived, nothing. No popcorn or lions. No ringmaster with a long whip strapped to his side. No trapeze, no high dive, no clowns, and no one being shot out of a cannon. Before we were saved, the preshow was exciting. But once we entered the big top, we found less pomp and more circumstance. We'd been had.

People still died even though we'd been told they wouldn't, our children still got sick even though we'd been told they wouldn't, we were still hated even though we'd been told we would be loved, and we were still abused even though we'd been told we would be protected. We were still afraid, lonely, and hopeless even though we had been told that Immanuel, "God *with* us," would never leave our side. Everything had been presented as cheese on a cracker, simple and tasty, but none of it was true.

To say this bait and switch was only a simple disappointment is a massive underestimate.

Some of us ignored the lie and pretended all the empty promises came true. We said it was God's will when someone died of cancer. We responded to each spiritual riddle with ease, creating a theological answer box with a little extra room for whatever new situation cropped up—an occasional suicide, a baby born with trisomy 13, genocide. But others of us marched in protest against the illusion that God was the answer.

So we told him to get out.

We tore the religious bumper stickers from our cars, stopped praying before meals, and found ourselves paralyzed when it came time to make a big ask of God, because our prior requests for life reform had been ignored. And even when there appeared to be a bit of mystical activity in the vicinity of our problem, it never fit inside the theological answer box provided because that box had already been filled with lies that had distorted our view of God.

How then were we to proceed with our faith?

We ran to our churches, pastors, and spiritual mentors to show them our findings but were told to settle down. Their implicit message skimmed over obvious discrepancies in the faith and focused on a narrow group of people who wanted only to be told how to marry well, finance well, raise kids well. We weren't taken seriously because they didn't know the answers themselves, and rather than wade into the mystery, they opted for ignorance and called it faith.

I understand the difficulty they faced. Parishioners wanted answers and were paying the pastor for exactly that, so the pressure was on. But they should have just leveled with us and said, "I don't have an answer for that," when they didn't have an answer for that.

I do believe that most of them were doing the best they could, but they must have felt like frauds. They had studied theology and filled their minds with information about God and yet, at the end of the day, had so little to show for themselves. They could tell you exactly where Capernaum was on a biblical map and could explain the lineage of David down to a T, but they couldn't tell you how the thief on the cross got into heaven when he never said the sinner's prayer. They were incapable of pulling back the celestial curtain— incapable of revealing the mysteries of the great and powerful Oz. So what was the point of their being pastors? They were no different than the rest of us. They were just as confused, just as broken, and just as in need of a rescue. But they never identified themselves as one of us even though we *needed* them to; they never told us the truth about their own hurts, habits, and hang-ups.

How could we not have felt alone and ashamed?

———————

According to the second book of Corinthians, Paul said, "I had this thorn and I couldn't get rid of it, even though I prayed and prayed and prayed. But the Lord said, 'My power is made perfect in weakness.' Therefore I will boast all the more gladly about my weaknesses, so that Christ's power may rest on me" (see 12:7–9). One chapter earlier Paul said, "I will glory of the things that concern my weakness" (v. 30 ASV).

The word *glory* is often defined as "the silent existence" or "the unspoken manifestation of God." The Greek word for glory is *doxa*, which is also used to convey God's intrinsic worth or his core value.

So not only is the glory of God *revealed* in our brokenness, in the ruins of our lives, in those things we can't figure out, get right, or seem to overcome, but his *core value* is at its absolute highest when we are at our absolute lowest. The silent existence of God is alive in my brokenness, where his power is not simply present but "made perfect."

Wow. I will *glory* of the things that concern my weakness.

In *The Four Loves*, C. S. Lewis says, "Friendship … is born at the moment when one man says to another 'What! You too? I thought that no one but myself …'"[1] It has been said that at the start of every healthy friendship are the words *me too*. There is enough power in those words to keep someone from going off the deep end, yet we are still prone to saying, "That's too bad for you," pitying our friends when our understanding is so desperately needed.

If someone confesses to cheating on his wife and I have cheated on my wife, it is best to say, "Me too," not "Wow, that's not good." Or if someone confesses she was abused as a child and I know something of that kind of darkness, saying, "Me too—you are not alone—we're the same," is so curative landing on the soul of the injured.

Last Saturday evening I sat in a Mexican restaurant with several old friends and a family of new friends from South Dakota. I didn't know the family well but had met Jim and Pat when they'd visited Indianapolis the year before. Their daughter Jamie sat across the table from me. Jamie is twenty-nine and the epitome of classic beauty with chestnut hair, pale smooth skin, and beautiful dark brown eyes that still manage to be bright.

Jamie has Huntington's disease, a progressive neurodegenerative disorder that is characterized by the destruction of nerve cells in specific areas of the brain. A noticeable side effect is palsy-like shaking, resembling Parkinson's disease. The shaking associated with Huntington's is measured numerically on a scale of 1 to 100. Jamie's logs in at 75, making it difficult to understand her speech at times. But because Jamie has become a self-confident woman in the midst of her suffering, she keeps at it until you understand her perfectly.

She hasn't always been so self-assured.

Jim and Pat adopted Jamie when she was a baby. It wasn't too long before they realized she wasn't like the rest of the family. Jamie was shy and introverted, preferring to have her nose in a book; the rest of the family was extroverted. But it went deeper than that. In fourth grade, a boy in Jamie's class called her Fatty, and when he did, something shifted significantly in her spirit and she was a goner. That one lie worked its way into her chest and she passionately believed it was true. As a result, anorexia and bulimia were inaugurated into her life and would stay with her for more than fifteen years. When Jamie reached rock bottom, she weighed eighty pounds and was taking up to sixty laxatives a day.

But anorexia and bulimia were not Jamie's only problems.

Diagnosed with bipolar disorder in her twenties, Jamie began cutting to relieve the anxiety brought on by her obsession to be perfect. With unrelenting suicidal thoughts, which accompanied what she believed was bipolar disorder, Jamie attempted to take her life several times. Her world was a daily plague of self-doubt and self-loathing. She saw no purpose in herself whatsoever.

Several years later, Jamie went on a mission trip with her family. While hiking the rain forests of Nicaragua, she began falling down repeatedly. Initially her family assumed it was only a side effect of the bipolar medication, but as it began happening often, her mom made a doctor's appointment to have Jamie examined. It was during this appointment that Jamie's doctor encouraged her to see a neurologist.

After a battery of tests, the neurologist gave her the news. It wasn't bipolar disorder. It had never been bipolar disorder. It was Huntington's chorea.

Huntington's chorea is fatal. Because it affects muscle control, in time it will either shut down Jamie's heart or prohibit her brain from sending messages to the organs that give her life. The most powerful side effect of Huntington's for Jamie will be the loss of her life.

Pat couldn't shake the feeling that she had let her daughter down. "When we adopted Jamie, we thought we were sparing her from something awful. When we received the Huntington's diagnosis, I cried for a month because there was this horrible sense that I had fallen short as her mother.

"We adopted her because she had no roots. We gave her *our* roots, but it wasn't enough. In fact, it had never been enough because she had always struggled, from her childhood right on into her twenties. We couldn't figure out what to do for her," she told me. "Something was missing for Jamie. Something had always been missing."

After receiving her diagnosis, Jamie wanted to know more about her medical history. She made an appeal, and the sealed documents from her adoption were opened. Within a few months, Jamie and Pat boarded a plane for Indiana to meet Jamie's biological mother.

"It was like looking in the mirror," Jamie told me, grinning from ear to ear. "She looked just like me." Pat listened intently as her daughter told me about the mom she had never known. Jamie had found something in her biological mother that not only made sense to her but also changed her—for good.

"She didn't come back the same. Everything she had struggled with—the anorexia, mood swings, self-hatred, lack of purpose in her life—all just disappeared. Completely."

"They did, they did," Jamie said, smiling at her mother. "I don't really know why, but they were gone, weren't they?"

In October of 2012, just four short months after the visit, Jamie's biological mother died—of Huntington's chorea.

Remember this moment, when your mother's
body heals every trouble of your soul.
—Anita Diamant, *The Red Tent*

Jamie had found her roots. She wasn't alone. She had company.

The suicidal thoughts and mood swings, the eating disorder and insecurities, all left her the day she met her birth mom. For the first time in her life, she was at peace. Jim and Pat had given Jamie their roots, but they couldn't give her a sound mind. She had to find this on her own, and she found it when she finally understood she was not alone.

I'm in awe of the courage it must have taken for her to board the plane that day—the courage to charge into the unknown.

And the end of all our exploring
Will be to arrive where we started
And know the place for the first time.

Jamie would tell you that "knowing the place" was knowing herself and that knowing herself saved her life.

There would still be difficulties along the way. Jamie's fiancé opted not to marry her because he wanted kids and Jamie had already decided not to carry on the Huntington's legacy. "I just couldn't do that to a child," she said empathetically. "There was no way I was going to put my babies through what I've been through."

She was equally compassionate with her fiancé. "I understood why he broke up with me. It would have been a lot for him to take all this on," she said, waving a hand over herself. I had to hold back the tears when she said this because all I saw was beautiful.

I was curious about Jamie's response to God. She was a writer, a deep thinker, and an introvert—someone who had seen the darker side, perhaps the *darkest* side, of life. I wanted to know if she was angry. I wanted to know how she felt about all of it.

"Do you have any questions for God?" I asked her.

She didn't hesitate to answer. "Not really. I had a lot of questions for him when I was young and struggling so much in life, but not now."

"So you and God, you're good?" I asked, giving her a second shot at him. But she didn't need one.

"Yeah. I'm not upset," she told me again. I hadn't known her prior to this night, but I couldn't imagine she'd ever been anything but this unruffled person sitting before me. It was difficult to comprehend how in the most debilitating time of her life, she could've been more herself and more at peace than she had ever been before.

Jamie didn't have a single question for God, but the incurable irony of her life was too much for me that night.

Where is God? I wondered. *Who is God?*

Austrian poet and novelist Rainer Maria Rilke once wrote,

I would like to beg you … to have patience with everything unresolved in your heart and to try to love the *questions themselves* as if they were locked rooms or books written in a very foreign language. Don't search for the answers, which could not be given to you now, because you would not be able to live them. And the point is, to live everything. *Live* the questions now. Perhaps then, someday far in the future, you will gradually, without even noticing it, live your way into the answer.[2]

This is what I love about God. And it's what I hate about him too. Sometimes I'm okay with the mystery, and then I'm not okay at all. But God's transcendental determinations are not made in a public forum. They are made in a private room where he alone is at work—where he alone watches over our lives. In the end, many of his spiritual mathematics just don't add up. Not that I want them to.

———————

Marcia Schwartz is the groundskeeper at my church and is deeply loved by all the staff. She has the gentlest spirit known to man. There are those rare few who seem to be incapable of meanness in any form. She is one of those people.

Our church participates in a program that works to rehabilitate teens who've gotten into a fair share of legal trouble. Marcia is always the first to request them. "Hey, these are good kids," she says with complete confidence and puts them to work digging holes, planting flowers, and mowing the yard. And just like the rest of our staff, the kids love her deeply. How could they not?

Most of the people who attend the weekend services at my church wear name tags, many of which end up either in the parking lot or strewn across the church lawn. When Marcia finds a name tag lying around, she picks it up and puts it in her pocket. All throughout the day, she prays for the person in her pocket. She may not know the individual, but to her that doesn't matter one bit.

Near the end of the workday, as Marcia packs up to go home, she pulls the name tags she's found from her pocket and puts each one in a special bucket in her shed. There are hundreds of name tags in her special bucket, and every once in a while she says a Massive Marcia Prayer for all of them.

"One day I prayed for this woman, and when I saw her later that week I told her I had prayed for her on Tuesday, because that's when I found her name tag in the parking lot. And guess what? Tuesday was her birthday," she says, giggling at God's secret plan. "Can you even believe that? I prayed for her *all day* on her *birthday*. What a privilege!"

Video stories are fairly common at my church, so when the topic of prayer was to be discussed during one of our weekend services, Marcia's was the obvious video to show. She is one of the most prayerful people I have ever known. But what I didn't know was how her desire to pray for others had come out of incredible pain and brokenness.

From the time Marcia was a little girl, her mother was mentally ill. Marcia would lie in bed at night and pray God would supernaturally heal her mom because she believed he could. She prayed that one simple request for a lifetime.

"Pray without ceasing" (1 Thess. 5:17 ESV) we've been told, but have we honestly understood what that means? For Marcia it simply means without ceasing—forever. So she prayed, without ceasing, that the burden of her mom's mental illness would eventually be lifted.

Several years ago, at the age of eighty, her mom became very ill and it was apparent she wasn't going to make it. Marcia's ceaseless prayers were still going strong. And then out of the blue, four months before she died, her mom received a spirit of love and a sound mind. For the next three weeks, she enjoyed complete and total mental clarity for the first time in her life.

"He healed her," she told me during her interview. "God healed my mom for those three weeks, and I was so happy! I was so happy because God answered my prayer. And I just know if he answered my prayer then, he will answer again. That's why I keep praying for people. Because God is so faithful and he answers the prayers of his people."

On that day, I believe the unspoken manifestation of God was alive in Marcia's brokenness.

I often think about Jamie's story—about how meeting her birth mother changed everything for her. "She didn't come back the same," Pat had told me.

On her flight home from Indiana, Jamie was already making new plans for her life. She felt a calling to tell her story. The fact that she had been to hell and back inspired her to say, "Me too."

But Jamie's "me too" didn't just drop out of the sky. She got on a plane and went searching for it. She packed her bags and went on a powerful journey to find it. And when she looked into the eyes of the woman from whom she had been knit together, that's when she found her "me too."

What if there was redemption in Jamie's disease? What if, while it was enslaving her physical body, it was capable of delivering others just like her, the way her mother's disease had delivered Jamie?

And what if Marcia's calling to pray, which was born of personal tragedy and ruin, had the power to change God's mind on something? You may think, *But how often is God's mind getting changed?* And I hear you. But whenever there is something I'm desperate to see made right in my life, Marcia is the first person I go looking for. Because deep down, beneath layers of unfaith and unbelief, I have faith in *Marcia's* faith. I believe in her calling to pray because I know it comes from the core ache within her.

And what about us? What if we could be called *to* something and *for* something that God needs *us* to make right in the world, just like these two courageous women?

If my broken story can be used for good in this world, then I believe it's true that my weakness is his glory. And I can only hope that the calling to change things for the good would stop at nothing to eradicate the ineffective and unproductive life I have chosen more times than I'd like to admit.

I am to be a broken vessel poured out among those unfortunate ones stuck in their own personal hell on earth, and because I already know something about hell on earth …

I will glory in my weaknesses, so that the power of Christ may rest upon me.

His glory might not bring the dead back to life, but his glory that is made perfect in my brokenness could bring the dead within others back to life. Will there still be questions without answers? Yes. But I don't think answers are what we are looking for anyway. I think we're looking for grace—enough so that we can manage the pain. And answers are not grace; they're just information. Empathy is grace. Company is grace.

"Me too." That's grace.

ME ENCANTA
The Love of God

When I was a kid, my favorite substitute teacher shaved a full beard.
She wore big gold brooches on the lapel of her pantsuits. She looked
just like Gabe Kaplan from Welcome Back, Kotter *and sang bass*
in a female choir called Sweet Adelines. She was the most unexpected
thing we had ever seen—as manly as our dads but as tender as our
grandmothers. With all that was happening in my adolescent years, I
needed to know I was worth something. Mrs. Banning made it clear
that I was. I loved her and knew that she loved me. I imagine God is
pleased when we allow the foolish things of this world to confound our
wisdom—when we allow ourselves to be drawn into his love in the
most peculiar ways. I won't forget Mrs. Banning, and I won't forget her
brooches either—big golden bees and hummingbirds, so feminine on
such a masculine woman. It was odd. She was odd. As odd as God.

When I was a junior at Anderson University, my Spanish professor,
Dr. Sid Guillen, had a stroke right there in the classroom. He was

lecturing on verb conjugation when I noticed he had conjugated a verb in the wrong tense. Because Spanish was Dr. Guillen's native tongue, this woke a few of us out of our higher-learning hypnosis. I looked up and saw a troubled look on his face.

"Mr. Guillen, are you okay?" I asked as he fell to his knees. Within seconds another student ran out of the classroom to call 911. By the time the ambulance arrived, several of us were gathered around him, stroking his hair and telling him everything was going to be okay. There were tear streaks like toboggan chutes down each side of his face, and fear was deeply set in his eyes as he mumbled gibberish to us in Spanish. Initially he tried coming back to class but suffered another stroke and had to call it quits for good.

It was odd not seeing Dr. Guillen in class. He was replaced by a man who was a complete snooze, and we missed Dr. Guillen terribly because he was full of surprises, kicking over desks when we weren't paying attention and breaking into loud Spanish love songs without warning. A couple of years ago, I read in our alumni newsletter that Dr. Guillen had passed away. The article said he had lived a long life and was surrounded by family when he died.

You get to thinking about the impression people leave on you after they die. Dr. Guillen once told us we should be taking his Spanish class very seriously even if it was only a core class. Why?

"Because Spanish is what they speak in heaven," he told us, "and you're going to want to be able to say more than just '¿Cómo te llamas?' to the Almighty when you get there." And he was right. Only being able to ask God his name might not be terribly impressive. So I listened to his advice and dug into my Spanish homework. I'm pleased to say that after taking two years of high school Spanish followed by one year in college, I'd be able to ask God not only his name but also for directions to the bathroom. And I could easily tell him I liked his dog. "*¡Me gusta tu perro, Jesús!*" So I think I'm in good shape.

This morning I watched a YouTube video that brought tears to my eyes. I've seen it before, but for some reason the music, the man's voice singing, and the pairing of the song with Pachelbel's Canon went straight through me. There are heavenly moments when everything comes into order and you have no trouble believing there is more out there. I had one of these moments the other day on a bike ride.

I rode into the little town of Westfield, Indiana, and then farther out into the country. Rows of corn lined the asphalt road as my tires buzzed against it. Sometimes I talk to the corn while I ride. "Hello, corn. You're beautiful this year," I say. It's odd, I'll admit, but I think it can hear me even though it never says a word.

I parked my bike on the side of the road and examined the way the corn shot out of the ground and how the leafy husk wrapped itself so tightly around the cob, protecting the kernels inside. And as I stood admiring each long regal limb, I had my moment. I felt God walking out to me from deep within the rows of corn. He almost never speaks to me anymore, but I don't worry about that at all. I used to beg him to tell me stuff—to answer my questions and tell me why for so many things I didn't understand, things I had decided to make him responsible for. But on this day, he stood quietly at my side as we admired the corn together.

"Hmm," I said. "Just beautiful."

"Yeah," he said back.

And in this fraction of a moment, my spirit didn't have to figure anything out—didn't have to know why for a thing. I carry moments like this with me. I have so many of them locked away in a special jar.

Another one of them was at the visitation for my brother's funeral. The room was filled with guests and stories were flying everywhere. It felt so much more like a family reunion than a funeral. And then it happened: I heard my mom.

A cry cut through the place and brought the room to a deafening silence. Several hundred of us stood by listening to the grieving howl as a mother's soul replaced the beautiful memory of her son's birth with his death. It was a song that until this day I had never heard. Her own death rang out among the living, killing us softly. And in her grief, I could hear God singing—singing of human collapse, of heartbreak and tragedy, where he is so easily found yet so casually dismissed. I didn't like his song one bit, but I heard it just the same and would have been a fool to pretend he wasn't strumming my pain with his fingers.

I've had the thought for quite some time of what it would be like to hear God sing. It was such a beautiful thought to me because I am a musician by trade. I imagined all the lovely voices I'd ever heard: the power of dramatic classical sopranos, the guts of black gospel singers, and the passionately organic voice of such singers as Annie Lennox all rolled into one. I could imagine the potential. I could visualize God's singing voice overwhelming all who heard it.

One day I picked up a CD in a music store and as I read through the song titles on the back cover, I saw "Imagine (How God Can Sing)." It was the very last song on the CD. I didn't hesitate. I purchased the CD immediately for that song title alone. Someone had finally done it—captured the idea of what it would be like to hear God sing. In it, I thought there might be a clue, some kind of insight into the God of the whole universe. And because I wanted to be in the know, I raced back to my office to give it a listen.

Sitting in my chair near the window that looked out over the parking lot, I peeled back the cellophane and popped the shiny new disc into the kind of machine you see only at garage sales anymore. I was expectant. It was the last track. Some of the best songs I've ever heard were last tracks. I thought about the last track on Cindy Morgan's *Listen* project and remembered how it haunted me the first time I heard it. I quickly forwarded the CD to track eleven. The song began and I sat quietly, staring out the window, hanging on every note and word.

I tried hard to take it in—the lyrics and the melody—but the song didn't pan out for me as I'd hoped it would. I expected a revelation but was left ambivalent. I felt cheated. Surely the songwriter must have known that a song about God singing needed to be something special—a whale call, forty-three harps being plucked at the same time, a helicopter blade chopping in the background. Needless to say, it wasn't inspiring. It was cliché. It happens. It might have overwhelmed someone else, but it didn't overwhelm me. I set the CD aside, complained to a couple of friends, and got over it.

The longer I live, the more I long for the clues and insights of life (or of God), yet I realize there are so many more things left unexplained than I ever thought there were in my twenties. In my twenties, God was obedient. In my thirties, he was an unruly child, whom I did my best to train up. And now in my forties, he is God and I am not. And his song is minor. There are short-lived moments when he sings in C major, but most often he sings outside the lines, adagio, because of the great skill and lyricism it requires to place each syllable dissonantly within the minor chords. His song is potent, not pretty. And it's only beautiful sometimes. It is anything but cliché.

I have felt peculiar in my forties, as though there is a crack in my heart. And the more time I spend with good spiritual people (you know the kind: biblically buttoned up, scripture verses on their coffee mugs), the more peculiar my heart, and the more I feel misshapen and out of place. I feel uncomfortable with those eager to punctuate their pain with an exclamation point before it's time. Instead my heart feels most at home with those who understand their pain and are comfortable putting an ellipsis where an ellipsis belongs, because so many things are left unredeemed.

My sister and Chuck came for a visit this past weekend. As soon as she climbed out of their truck, I could see the effects of the chemo. Her body was not her body. She had gained quite a bit of weight from the steroids, and her face was no longer the shape of my father's face, as it always had been. It was swollen and odd. A friend of mine who was a nurse told me not to look at Trina with "the death stare," so I decided that if I needed a moment to gather myself throughout the weekend, I would escape to my closet or go sit in the backseat of my car, both of which I ended up doing several times.

This morning, as Trina was getting ready to leave, I sat on the toilet in our guest bathroom and watched her put on her makeup just as I had when I was a little boy.

"What's that stuff?" I asked her.

"Brightener," she told me. "It gets rid of any darkness under my eyes."

"You're so pretty," I told her. She smiled.

She pulled out eyebrow pencils and focused intently to make sure she got her brows just right in the absence of her own. She had shaved her hair off several weeks earlier because it was getting patchy, but it had since grown about an inch or so. It was the softest hair I had ever felt, although it had almost no color to it at all. I called her Baby Hair several times over the weekend and kissed the top of her head as if she really were a baby. She would smile and giggle at her new nickname.

I had a group of friends gather while she was in town to pray for Trina's healing. We collected our love and prayers around her and as we prayed, tears streamed down her face and ours.

Afterward, while everyone waited their turn to talk to her, I over-heard her tell a friend of mine that not having hair was great for riding on the back of Chuck's motorcycle because she didn't have to worry about how she looked when she took off her helmet. It was what I had always loved about her: her ability to believe the best in any situation. And even with the room littered with cancer, threatening her life, showing itself in her warped body, swollen face, and hair loss, her sense of hope hadn't changed one bit. She put on her makeup just as she always had, as if she were just as gorgeous as she had always been. These things—these incredible things—I pick them up and put them in my jar.

I watched her like a hawk the entire weekend, taking in all the beauty that she is, not able to think of one thing I hadn't liked about her before. I saw her eat a bowl of vanilla ice cream heaped with

Banana Split Oreos she had crumbled on top. She "mmmm'ed" over each bite as if God had pulled the recipe straight from his own stash of cooking magazines. "Hit me again," she said when her bowl was nearly empty, and I did.

I realized over the weekend that I might know her better than anyone ever has. We had come up in the same family, drawn together as survivalists in the war zone. And as survivors often do, we had formed a bond that would never be broken. I was the first one she called after she made the painful decision to leave her husband of twenty-nine years. On the phone that day, I asked her if she was leaving before she ever mentioned it herself, because I could already hear it in her voice. Because I know her.

We talk on the phone four or five times every week, talking about nothing because we don't need anything to talk about. We make our way in the conversation without material because enough has already happened. She is not replaceable as my sister. The thought of losing her is absurd.

I am writing this too early to know what will happen to her. And if she passes, I don't know what will happen to me. It is impossible to gauge whether I will completely fall apart or discover some kind of new strength, which I don't want if it only means losing her. As far as God is concerned, I have gone down this road before. I have lashed out, *un*believed in him, accused him, and sworn to back out of any deal I'd made with him. But in the end, I have found him capable of restoring my faith because he knows me better than I even know my sister. He's shown up, amid the visceral pain, in powerful ways I could not excuse, leaving me fully aware that he'd been there. I can't possibly begin to know that I will always believe him, love him, forgive him, let him in, but so far, in the midst of the most difficult personal circumstances, he has not left me.

He hasn't answered all of my questions, and he certainly hasn't "worked all things out for the good" in any way I would've expected. But once when I was at an all-time low, he entered into my broken world so unexpectedly and in a way that was so tangible even my peculiar heart couldn't deny his presence. This heavenly encounter and the personal gift he arrived with will forever remain in my jar.

And still there have been other times when he showed up with only a quiet whisper into my spirit yet fully revived these dried-up bones. He used foolish things like cornfields and bike rides, like my wife and her witty sense of humor that can clear my sorrow away like a leaf blower. Things like my two girls, one whose faith in people I've come to depend on, always making a way for even the worst of all pirates, including me. And the other who has her mother's sense of humor and can manage to make me laugh until tears fill my eyes, completely blurring out my troubles. In these moments, all is well. I feel loved by something. And more than that, I feel comforted, empathized with. I wish I could hold on to this all the time, but it comes and goes and then comes again, sometimes just after I have escaped into my closet or the backseat of my car.

Sometimes it feels as if God has invited himself into *my pain*, when I had hoped to be invited into *his healing*. We want a God who heals our wounds, but it seems we have a God who heals our hearts. My expectation was that he would make the pain leave me—that if the pain were little birds nesting in my heart, he would know when it was time for them to go and he'd toss them out of me. But some of them never fly away.

It's not okay. These birds weren't meant to nest in me; they were supposed to soar right on past me, beating their wings until I couldn't see the threat of them anymore. But their wings were clipped, and for reasons I don't understand, they wound up in my heart. As I said, it's not okay. It will never be okay. But there they are, just the same. And I have felt that if God were truly God, he would shoo them away or starve them off until they died one by one. But for those things that have been left unredeemed, pain can be a lifetime mortgage. I will pay on it, and I can learn to manage it, but it's not going anywhere. Yet it will not be *all* that is me. It does not complete me. While it remains, God also will remain. And I will find him in the ruins, among three thorns and three prayers for their removal. He will provide his compathy and care with cornfields and bike rides and laughter and love—especially love.

If my sister doesn't survive her fight with cancer, I will be wrecked, and I won't pretend I shouldn't be. I will tell God what a liar he is and shake my fist at him for all the bad things that happen. I will tell others he's a fraud and that he kills the people other people need. I will walk my cul-de-sac in protest. I may even abandon him.

But then I imagine he will do what he always does. In some unexpected way, he will show up—show up for me, and in *your* pain, show up for you. And together we'll find him. We will find God in the ruins.

———————

After watching the YouTube video that so moved me this morning, I looked down to see the remarks others had written about it. There were several, but my eyes focused on one: "Me encanta." It was one of the few Spanish phrases I could still recall from Dr. Guillen's class. Someone had watched the same video, and I imagine had a moment for which they had written only two words: "Me encanta."

I love.

Those things left unredeemed in us are unfinished stories we're desperate to punctuate, hoping to turn the page and see "The End." But tragedy will always be with us, as will disbelief, fear, abandonment, and the abysmal injustices we see every time we turn on the television. At times the adversity and pain of this world have siphoned off whatever belief was left in me. But then I go to my jar, and I remember the corn in Westfield, how its long regal limbs pressed themselves up toward the heavens. Or I conjure up the image of my dearly beloved sister, riddled with cancer from head to toe, talking about the benefits of not having hair as if even the storm cloud that is cancer has a silver lining. Or I close my eyes and hear the terribly holy song I heard God singing in my mother's grieving howl at my brother's funeral, and I don't hear unbelief at all or even death. Instead I hear two words: "Me encanta." I don't know why I hear them, but I know I can't shake them. And truth be told, I don't want to. They are imprinted into the spiritual DNA of who I am, and they speak to my tragedies, my doubts, and my personal failures.

Time and time again, I hear them called out to me in the tiniest voice—a voice so small it could fit only within the most peculiar crack of my heart.

Me encanta. Me encanta. Me encanta.

I love.

PART 3

STORYTOLD

THE UNTOLD STORY—I USED TO BE MATT PETRINO

The Power of Your Story

There is no greater agony than bearing an untold story inside you.

—Maya Angelou

I was in the market for new shoes. Shoes are everything in fourth grade; they can make or break you. In fourth grade, the right shoes just might catapult you into the future with enough torque to broaden your list of potential prom dates to include the likes of Robin Larabee.

There was a house in the "old money" portion of our subdivision and I needed some old money to buy a new pair of shoes. The house had a huge lawn that was terribly overgrown and the flower beds were in pretty bad shape. Every once in a while I would see an old lady picking around in them, so one day I stopped to see if she needed help.

"Want me to mow your lawn?" I called out to her. She was on all fours, digging through weeds and fifteen-year-old mulch. I could tell she didn't hear me, so I cupped my hands around my mouth and yelled as loud as I could: "Hey, lady! Do you want your lawn mowed?"

She stood up and turned around. At barely five feet tall and less than a hundred pounds, she was nothing but breath and britches.

She waved me over, so I got off my bike and made my way through her long grass. The first thing I noticed was that she was wearing bowling shoes with large number sixes painted on the back of them. Part of her hair was jet black, but when she took off her sun hat, the rest was stark white with a line of demarcation four or five inches from her scalp. Some of her teeth were missing, the back ones mostly, but her smile lit up the rest of her face.

"Yes," she said, "I would. And I'll give you ten dollars to do it." Her bright pink lipstick was gooped around her mouth as though she'd put it on in her sleep.

Ten dollars was big money for lawn mowing. She must not have known the going rate because I got only five for all my other lawns. What a dummy. But two days later, I was still mowing. There were hidden parts to her yard that couldn't be seen from the street. And because it hadn't been mowed since Jimmy Carter was inaugurated, I could barely make it through one strip without having to empty the bag. On the second day of mowing, Tim came down to help. We split the cash. Two days of mowing for five dollars. Who's the dummy?

The word on the street was that Mrs. Poor (I kid you not) was filthy rich. So when she started calling our house to see if "the boys" could come down and give her a hand with a few odd jobs, we were all about it. And that's how we became The Handyboys.

Before too long, I began to wonder if Mrs. Poor was mentally ill. The thought was confirmed the day I saw her pulling weeds in the middle of July while wearing a fur coat. Although mental illness was already a part of my life (Stepdad from Hell), Mrs. Poor's variety of mental illness was different. It was much less complicated and kept its distance, so I didn't really mind it.

Her house was a wreck inside, and some days she would still be in bed when we checked on her after school. But then with that big grin of hers she'd say, "Anyone up for some Jell-O?" She didn't cook much, but there were ten or fifteen Tupperware containers in the refrigerator that were filled with red, orange, and lime-green Jell-O.

After we had known Mrs. Poor for about a month, we received a phone call from her son, Ronald, whom we didn't even know existed. He said he appreciated all the ways The Handyboys were helping his dearly beloved mother. (For free, by the way. We couldn't find her safe anywhere in that house.) He also said that if we continued to mow the yard and care for her house, he'd "remember us come Christmas." I'll spare you the dramatic wait. We got nothing. Actually, he did send a Christmas card. And as my mom opened it, we gathered around and held out our hands so all the cash would fall directly into our lawn-mowing, snow-shoveling, weed-pulling, window-washing, Jell-O–making hands. But Ronald was a liar. We'd been had. That'll teach you to help old ladies.

Mrs. Poor had a pill dispenser in her basement that automatically dispensed her medication several times a day. On one particular visit, she was in full meltdown mode because it hadn't delivered the goods. She was screaming for her meds, and we didn't know what to do. (Might we just pause for a moment and ask ourselves where social services was in the 1980s?) She told us the pill dispenser was broken, but we didn't believe her, so we stood by waiting for her meds to come down its snout. Nothing. We could hear Mrs. Poor crying from upstairs, "I need my pills—I've got to have those *blankety-bleeping* pills!" Talk about stress. But I had a plan.

Because my wrists were smaller than Tim's, I wedged my arm up the opening of the pill dispenser as though it were a vending machine, grabbing as if my life depended on it. Still nothing.

Tim came up with plan B. Yes, he got bad grades in school, but he was street smart. So when he said, "Here's what we're gonna do," I was all ears.

He picked up a pool stick from Mrs. Poor's pool table and began digging at the tip with his fingers. "What are you doing?" I asked, but he didn't answer. I could see he was prying the tip cover off. "Seriously, Tim, what are you doing?"

"What does it look like I'm doing? I'm trying to get the tip off."

"Why? What's wrong with it?"

"Nothing's wrong with it. I'm gonna feed it to her." He was dead serious.

"Okay, wait a second. What exactly do you mean by *feed*?" I asked, hoping this was all going to make sense.

"I mean I'm going to see if she'll eat it," he said as if he'd done this all before.

"Are you crazy?"

"I'm not crazy. *She's* crazy. That's why I'm gonna see if she'll eat this thing."

"Ooohhh, you mean like it's medicine." I was beginning to follow his train of thought. "Okay, well, *that* is not going to work," I said, pointing at the tip cover, "so let's try to find something that looks a little more like medicine." And I begin searching the basement floor for a stray piece of cat food, dog food, an old box of Tic Tacs—anything that was actually meant to be eaten.

"This is round," he said, finally getting the tip off, "like a pill. It'll be fine."

"And you think she's not gonna know she's eating the tip off a pool stick?"

"She thinks those bowling shoes are gardening shoes, doesn't she?"

He had a point.

We walked the tip of the pool stick up the stairs as if it were an unpinned grenade. I thought we might find Mrs. Poor standing on the roof of the house by now, but she was lying down in her bedroom.

Tim held the tip out to her, and neither of us said a word. I thought this was perhaps the dumbest thing we'd ever done. "Here you go, Mrs. Poor. You need to take this," he said as if he was Doogie Howser.

Mrs. Poor looked in his hand and then up at the two of us. "What's that supposed to be?"

"It's your medicine," he answered in full-blown baby talk. I could feel the sweat beading up on my forehead.

Mrs. Poor stood up, took the tip of the pool stick from his hand, examined it from all angles, and said, "I'm gonna need some water." So the three of us made our way to the kitchen. And as she stood there in a bright yellow raincoat, which I'm pretty sure she thought was a bathrobe, he fed it to her—just like he said he would. And that was that. She was as good as new.

She was. Me? I wish it were that simple.

I have so rarely felt that I wasn't going to go off the deep end or have a complete mental breakdown at some point. It was just a matter of time. For years I white-knuckled it, hoping I would last or that God would resurrect the dead in me if only seconds before I robbed a bank or stripped myself naked and walked down the middle of a highway. Like Mrs. Poor, I was a mess but nobody knew it.

A few months after eating the tip off that pool stick, Mrs. Poor mysteriously disappeared from her house without a word and we never saw her again. In her absence, Ronald had left us the key to her house. We continued caring for her lawn and made lots of Jell-O while she was away, but we missed her.

Before we ever met Mrs. Poor, there were at least fifty rumors we had all heard about her. One was that her husband was a successful doctor who had come home drunk after work one night. People said he drove his car straight through their garage door and ended up dead in the ravine behind their house. There was a demolished car lying on its side in the ravine, which gave the story a little more weight. In the summer, we'd hike to it and look for Mr. Poor's bones. One time we thought we had found a jawbone, which only added fuel to the fire of our stories.

There were also rumors that Mrs. Poor threw elaborate dinner parties in her home when she was young, inviting the wealthiest socialites in my hometown. I even heard she was once very beautiful and wore only the most expensive clothing. Part of this I knew was true because she had an entire closet filled with fur coats and matching fur hats that Tim and I paraded around in once she'd gone away.

But there was one rumor that made me sad. Some said the reason Mrs. Poor had gone insane was because one of her children had died during infancy and she had never recovered. This one felt truer than all the others, and whenever the neighborhood kids laughed about it, I felt a little sick inside.

Her house was put up for sale at the end of summer and a new family moved in by fall. Every time I rode my bike past her house, I pictured her in my mind. She always looked the same: goopy bright pink lipstick and size 6 bowling shoes. I liked her that way. I still like her that way. To this day I have no idea what her story was, but I know she had one.

We all do.

Often, mentally ill people aren't able to hide their stories as well as the rest of us. But I was good at hiding my story, because in order to keep things looking presentable on the outside, I knew exactly which parts needed to be left out: the abuse, the secrets, the lies. I had always intended to leave my story untold so that one day it might be shelved in the "out of print" section of life's library and never heard from again. But the truth is, after a while our untold stories begin telling our deepest secrets without our permission. They push their way into the world revealing one broken chapter after another, threatening to exchange the life we've always wanted with the life we've always feared.

I wish there were a maid for the abused—that she would gather her mops, dustpans, and disinfectants and scrub us down every time the filthy memories were resurrected within us. We have a long memory, the abused. And not only do the memories linger, playing out the broken scenes of our lives like a sadistic encore, but often they work us like a puppet in the here and now until we discover there is much more to *who we are* than just the abuse we've suffered.

The life I always wanted was the one with purpose, calling, and meaning, while the life I always feared was the terminal brokenness I thought would never go away. But how was I supposed to get the one with meaning and find purpose in the ruins of my life? There had to be a way. I needed to be rescued.

In high school, I excelled in music. My name was Matt Petrino back then. In fact, Petrino was my last name until I was eighteen years old. I can still write it on a piece of paper and it doesn't look strange to me at all.

Band, choir, and drama club were all that mattered to me between 1985 and 1989. Music was a break from my life—a chance to create something beautiful.

I recently met an old high school buddy for lunch, and he asked me (somewhat covertly) if our choir director ever "did anything" to me. I knew exactly what he meant. It was common knowledge that our choir director had molested quite a few students in my class, although none of us knew it then. I'm sure I would've been easy prey in those days, so I'm grateful he never laid a hand on me. In fact, the better angels of his nature had actually inspired me in my music.

I remember seeing him wipe tears from his eyes when I sang, "Your hands lie open in the long fresh grass." He met me in the hallway after my performance, put his hands on my shoulders, and with tears in his eyes nodded his head in approval. He didn't have to say a word. I knew he thought there was something special within me, and I needed the approval of this child molester for everything the other child molester had taken from me.

I can't understand the paradox of the awful kind of people who have bits of beauty in them. The idea (the audacity really) that God would use the artistic outlet of music coupled with a pedophile choir director to confirm the value of my life is unimaginable. God is either immensely creative or a complete sociopath. At times I've wondered. But if you can believe it, that choir-teaching child molester wound up in my jar and reminds me to this day that my life has great value.

It seems God used what was available at the time, and I'm glad he did—not only so I could know that my life had value but also so I could instill that same sense of worth into other broken people who came across my path.

I recently spoke to a fourteen-year-old girl who through tears said, "I feel like my family is going crazy." There was panic in her eyes. I could hear her real concern: *I feel like* I'm *going crazy.*

"They may be, sweetheart, but that doesn't mean you have to go with them," I told her. "One day you are going to have your own life, and you can make it whatever you want it to be."

I could sense relief coming into her spirit as her shoulders slid back down. Her face was powdered with hope.

It felt good to look her in the eyes and affirm her value apart from the dysfunction in her life. Ten years ago I would've thrown a few clichés at her or said her family wasn't really crazy, causing her to feel more alone in her reach for help than ever. But seeing her fourteen-year-old face receive the same truth I so desperately needed to know at her age was everything to me.

Yes, I know what the odds are. And yes, I realize that insanity begets insanity just like controlling begets controlling and addiction begets addiction. But I also believe in recovery, because I have seen the worst of all cases live in ways so different from who they used to be. I once knew a man shipwrecked on the island of racism who swam thousands of miles to find his freedom. Immersed in only the waters of tolerance at first, in time, acceptance and humility would create a wake behind him and follow him right to Love's shore.

People can change.

When I was eighteen years old, I walked into the courthouse in my hometown of Elyria, Ohio, and had my name legally changed back to my biological father's last name. That day I became Matt Bays. The judge sitting across the table from me asked why I wanted to change it.

"Because the stepdad who adopted me is a monster," I told him with great conviction. "And I want nothing to do with him."

"Then let's *do* this," he said. And without another word he pulled a hopeful pen from his desk drawer and signed the papers that gave me a new name and a new life—or so I thought.

I'm sure his signature had delivered women from abusive relationships and placed neglected children into good homes, transforming the lives of hundreds of people, but it didn't transform mine. It changed my name, but it didn't change me. Not one word in the earlier chapters was different.

Holocaust survivor Samuel Pisar said, "We may not live in the past, but the past lives in us."[1] I couldn't agree more. I was no longer Matt Petrino, but Matt Petrino was still living inside me—and he always will. Because the past survives.

I left the courthouse that day not knowing that a part of me would always be Matt Petrino. I desperately tried to shake him, and when I couldn't, I found a way to accept him and eventually be grateful for all he had survived on my behalf. As it turns out, he was quite the warrior. And because of his survival, I have been able to share my untold story with those who have needed to know they are not alone.

Elie Wiesel, a political activist and survivor of a Jewish concentration camp, said, "I decided to devote my life to telling the story because I felt that having survived I owe something to the dead.... And anyone who does not remember betrays them again."[2]

We must never forget all that we've overcome. It's easy to ignore our stories or disregard their power to call the hurting, wounded, and abused out of their hiding places. Looking back can be painful, especially if it feels as though you've read the broken passages too many times already. But if you continue turning the pages and inviting others to read along, you will find the grace of God beautifully on display in your storytold.

DEFAULT SETTINGS
Accepting Who You Are

Often, it's not about becoming a new person, but becoming the person
you were meant to be, and already are, but don't know how to be.
—Heath L. Buckmaster, *Box of Hair*

It's probably time to tell you the truth about me—that something
hopeful took up residence in me the day I was born. I recently saw
Dolly Parton in an interview saying, "My mother always told me I
was born with a happy heart."[1] I feel the same. I don't know how it
got there, but I'm reasonably sure it is part of my hardwiring. I'd be
lying if I said I wasn't glad it was there. I have not found my happy
heart to be bothersome when the disappointments of life come.
And even though it tells a lot of half-truths, I still believe that its
intentions are good, and I'm glad it can look at a bad situation and
struggle to see how it will last forever.

I've known plenty of people who are not wired like I am. They
assess a situation based on facts and not on the "could be" and most

of the time formulate a response that has no music to it. I'm glad
I know, work with, struggle through, and celebrate life with these
people. They keep people like me from turning every crisis of life
into a melodramatic movie scene where everything works out perfectly just before the credits roll.

I've also known people who can't seem to get out of their heads.
The drabbest parts of their lives are continually in their sight line and
they struggle to look away. They seem to unintentionally drag their
fear and frustration everywhere they go. They are not always the ones
with the worst story but often feel as though things will not work out
for them. And even when things do, they don't buy it; they're still
waiting for the shoe to drop.

Our genetic makeup, the melted butter of our predisposition
reaching into every nook and cranny of our souls, is not something
we can sop up with a napkin. I have come to believe that our character traits can be only slightly modified. It seems that this is who we
are, like it or lump it. Yet time and time again, those with a spring
in their step are put on a pedestal, while those typecast as an Eeyore
feel desperate to change themselves into a Tigger. But the expectation
that they will exchange their metaphorical lump of coal for a sack of
candy one day is rubbish.

Mandy was a freshman in college when I was a junior. She was
bubbly with blonde hair and an enormous smile. Her voice was as
delicate as Snow White's, and sparrows flitted around her everywhere
she went. She made her way through our college cafeteria at every
meal, stopping at table after table to bear witness to the beauty of
life, always with that enormous smile and bouncy blonde hair. I had
trouble picturing Mandy ever having a bad day.

Christmas break came and went, and with it so did the Mandy we all knew. She still made her rounds in the cafeteria, but her blonde hair had been dyed dark brown, she'd swapped voices with a depressed telemarketer, and her bright white teeth were trapped inside a mouth they were no longer a fit for.

This new persona just wasn't Mandy. She was harsh and negative. She no longer twirled her hair and giggled bubbles. Her eyes were half-mast, her voice a thundercloud, and her typical "Hello, everyone!" replaced with "I just got busted for not turning in a homework assignment." But before long, Mandy's blonde hair made a comeback, and her voice, though never quite as delicate as before, came out of the swamp and lived in the city. Mandy was her old self again and all was right with the world. I'm sure that wherever she is today, she uses her car horn only for waving at the neighbors.

Mandy couldn't pull off the introspective contemplative any more than Joaquin Phoenix could pull off the predictable conformist. Hardwiring cannot always be tampered with, and maybe it doesn't need to be. Maybe we are what we are for a reason—each playing our part while not realizing how important that part might be in the grand scheme of things.

But not everyone would agree with me. David Foster Wallace wouldn't.

David Foster Wallace was an acclaimed novelist, winning accolades in his twenties for his lengthy and complex writing. The literary world was waiting for the next big thing, and David was it. They loved him. In his thirties, he wrote the book *Infinite Jest*. At 1,079 pages, it solidified him as a writer who wasn't going away. Very important people believed that David's primal wisdom just might get us back to something infinite.

In 2005 David gave the commencement address at Kenyon College, a school known for academic achievement. Part of that speech went viral and for good reason: it encouraged us to rise above our own default settings, because in them we often fail to recognize how the doldrums of life (waiting in line at the grocery store, sitting in traffic, or dealing with irritating people) are a part of the greater story.

A portion of what David told us to do I agree with. He challenged us to think more when we are living in the lethargy or catching our stride in the "rat race" and to realize that we are not the center of the universe—that everyone does not need to get out of our all-important way. But there was also something in his commencement speech that felt wrong, as though he were missing something. I could feel his attempt to convince us that we could all be something else, perhaps someone different than who we are at our core. But core is core, even for David. And as he reasoned and implored the students of Kenyon College not to get caught up, I could feel David's default settings lurking just offstage, waiting for him to finish so they could welcome him back to his own personal rat race.

The portion of David's speech that went viral is called "This Is Water." Millions of people have watched it and felt the "Yes!" this type of video inspires. But in it, I kept hearing the subtle message "You're not enough. You should be more." That those of us who are not Gandhi, Nelson Mandela, or Mother Teresa have less worth—and in the wrong hands, the wrong soul, that kind of message can be terminal. His words cast the kind of shadow our unattainable expectations live and make empty plans in. They told us we will finally matter when we can rise above our default settings and become something else—some*one* else.

Because of all that happened with my brother as a child, I've felt terminally unique my whole life. All I ever wanted was to be from a family where everything was normal. It didn't have to be the Cleavers. I would have settled for *Diff'rent Strokes* but wound up with *Breaking Bad*. And when I came to the realization that I was from a broken home, I decided I wasn't going down without a fight, so I dressed and acted the part of the kid who came from a good family with a shiny past. And when that didn't work, I tried being the kid with a terrible childhood who, against all odds, had overcome and was finally just like the kid from a good family with a shiny past. But that didn't work either. And that's when I thought I just might die, because redemption seemed like a cruel joke—a full-on hoax.

What I didn't know was that it was going to be okay. In time I came to accept that I wasn't a man who grew up shiny—that my life's purpose wasn't to be polished gold but rather to identify the *fool's* gold and stop trying to be something I wasn't. My desire to override my default settings needed a healthy dose of reality. Change is most definitely a good thing, but at some point we need to close the "alternate settings" tab before we check every item on the list and give ourselves the kind of false hope that can become destructive.

"You can be whatever you want to be." Yes, I know. I say it to my girls. And I agree with the spirit of the idea. "Dream, achieve, work hard, and believe." These are all good things. But some dreams will not manifest because they can't. *But they did for Heidi Klum and Kanye West, so why not for me?* There are a myriad of reasons: gifting, discipline, location, location, location. And even if you were to overcome your limitations for a time, you would most likely come back to your default settings at some point, and when that happens, you won't have a recording contract for one reason alone—*because you can't sing.* So as it turns out, maybe you can't be whatever you want.

But we are affected by this dilemma far beyond talent, looks, or our ability to make money.

You might struggle with self-love because your mother never loved herself. You might need more approval than you should because you were never told you were enough. You might not let yourself off the hook for making an honest mistake because every time you try to, you hear your father's voice in your head saying, "If you were really sorry, you wouldn't have done it." Or you may spend all your intimate energy in front of the computer screen because it's the only place you don't feel the anxiety of being rejected.

When the damage of the past still affects us in the present, we pull up the "alternate settings" tab and start checking the boxes. We want things to be different. *We* want to be different. I believe this recurring twinge within us can become manageable, but I don't believe the deeper ache in our spirits (from which the twinge stems) will ever be torn out by the roots completely. And maybe, just maybe, that is okay.

On an episode of *Celebrity Rehab with Dr. Drew*, I watched Jason Davis—grandson of a billionaire, heir to a massive oil fortune, and severe heroin addict—finally come to grips with the truth of his default settings. Dr. Drew and a fellow counselor asked Jason what it was that he wanted. He said he wanted a dad he could turn to … And then came the alarming and painful truth from Dr. Drew: "You don't have that; you don't get that."[2]

This scene broke my heart, and it broke Jason's. He can find a way to *re*-parent himself by letting the love of others into his life and accepting the guidance of mentors who have his best interest at heart. But the man who should have been there when Jason was a boy wasn't. It can't be undone. Healed? Yes. Rewritten from this day forward? Yes. Undone? No. It is a part of who he is and always will be. Acknowledging this truth could actually set him free, but if he continues down this road of tampering with his default settings, he is only playing with fire. David Foster Wallace hinted at this in his speech:

> Think of the old cliché about "the mind being an excellent servant but a terrible master." This, like many clichés, so lame and unexciting on the surface, actually expresses a great and terrible truth. It is not the least bit coincidental that adults who commit suicide with firearms almost always shoot themselves in the head. They shoot the terrible master. And the truth is that most of these suicides are actually dead long before they pull the trigger.[3]

Only once in my life did I hold hands with Suicide. Looking back, Suicide felt more my friend in that dark moment than my actual friends. It had pulled me into a foxhole, I thought to rescue me. But once it had me there, instead of teaching me how to dodge the shrapnel whizzing at my soul, it told me there was no way out of that hole.

The truth? Suicide was not a friend to me. It was a coward—a sociopath that knew nothing of redemption. It huddled next to me in the foxhole, whispering lies right into my ear. But if you listen long enough, sometimes even a liar will tell you the truth. And eventually it did: "You're right, Matt. You will never be anything other than what you are right now. You can change, make something of yourself, even become worthwhile, but the fundamental *who* you are will always be there. You will always be you."

It was the last thing I wanted to hear. It was what had me sitting in an empty field in the first place, contemplating cutting my wrists so I could be a *new* me somewhere else.

But twenty-two years later, I realize Suicide was right, because I am still the same guy. I've changed, grown, shed some of my skin, even made something of myself, but the fundamental *who* I am has not changed and likely never will. I will always be me. And you will always be you. This truth, although painful at times, can also be liberating because we can finally stop running. We can finally stop chasing after the person we will never be.

I'm grateful this suicidal moment passed. It doesn't for everyone. It didn't for David Foster Wallace.

After listening to David's speech, out of curiosity I looked him up on *Wikipedia*. Right beneath his name, just before his list of accomplishments, was the date of his birth followed by the date of his early death.

David didn't "shoot the terrible master"; instead he hung himself in his home on September 12, 2008. He was forty-six years old. "Most of these suicides are actually dead long before they pull the trigger," he'd said just three years earlier. Few probably understand these grave words the way David did. Something internal was terribly broken within him. And just like my sweet friend Becky, before his life story was complete, David Foster Wallace ran out of ink.

We can never be certain as to why David Foster Wallace took his life or why anyone does, but at some level we know that these unfortunates do not feel at home within themselves. For us to move forward in this life or even survive, we must accept that this is who we are. We must come to terms with the idea that we are enough, today, exactly as we are.

I am and always will be me. There are parts I'd like to carve out with a knife even if it left me hobbling the rest of my life. And there are moments I'm so overwhelmed by who I'm *not* that if I were doing my carving then, I fear there'd be nothing left of me. But maybe we are all a little more alike than we think. And if that's true, maybe we ought to stop trying to alter our default settings and instead do what we can to accept that who we are at our core is exactly who we were always meant to be.

In one of author Thomas Merton's final poems, he says that in our search, desire, and aim to become all the things the world has expected of us, our serenity is renounced. Can you feel it? The expectations you might never live up to? To be this, to heal that, to overcome these things, to be redeemed in a particular way that erases any memory of what you've done, been through, or suffer from? But for the one who lets these idealistic expectations go, "it was a lucky wind that blew away his halo with his cares, a lucky sea that drowned his reputation."[4] Merton believed it was the ordinary who would find freedom—that the ordinary would inherit the earth.

> You're blessed when you're content with just who you are—no more, no less. That's the moment you find yourselves proud owners of everything that can't be bought. (Matt. 5:5 THE MESSAGE)

As a person of recovery, I certainly believe we can rewrite our stories and most definitely change the ending, but we cannot change the beginning and we cannot change the author. *We* are the authors, and every word in the story of our lives, from this day forward, is written by us. Undoubtedly God can create a plot twist as he did for Dorothy by sending a tornado, or if we get into trouble he can make it snow so the poppies won't lull us to sleep forever, but he is not writing our lives.

God will sharpen our pencils and even give us a clean sheet of paper if we mess things up. But when it's time to start writing, he will always put the pencil in *our* hands. Surely God is the author of life itself, but of *my* life God is not the author: he is the editor.

SOMEONE ELSE'S STORY
Telling Your Story

*Lies are handed down from generation to generation,
and those who've come before us often have
expectations that we will keep their secrets and lies
once they're gone. If we continue to corroborate
their forever fiction, their ghosts will be free to roam
within us and steal the native narrative of our souls.*

Memory is powerful. I still remember the Earth shoes my second-grade teacher wore over thirty years ago, mostly because she ran races with us at recess. And to our surprise, she was fast. Really fast.

I've always remembered insignificant details, such as Crystal Barrington's crooked bangs or Terry Temple's chapped lips, but it took me longer to remember the more important parts of my life. And even when I did, I had to shut my eyes and listen closely to the dysfunctional pattern of my own heartbeat before I knew for sure which things had affected me.

"I promise to tell the truth, the whole truth, and nothing but the truth." In a court of law, people raise their hand and swear to tell the truth. But the truth is not easy, not because we are liars but because it's easier to tell a version of the truth. So when it was time for me to tell the truth, I got out the scissors and cut things out of the family pictures that I didn't want to remember, censoring the images of my story that I believed were inappropriate. But the truth is never inappropriate.

Parts of my story had always pointed a finger in my direction, holding me responsible for what had happened. When I could no longer handle the accusations, I grabbed a pencil and rewrote the scenes that made me look bad so I wouldn't lose my dignity. I needed the darker scenes to be more palatable—for you, for my therapist, perhaps even for myself.

I sat across from Doug in my counseling appointments and was fully capable of owning the incest with my brother. Accepting what it meant about me was another story. I could talk about it—I knew the details, even the smells—but when Doug asked the simple question, "What did the incest with your brother mean about you?" I was paralyzed.

"Nothing," was my first answer, followed by, "I guess I don't really understand what you're getting at."

"I'm not getting at anything. I'm just asking if you believed the incest meant something about you. You guys were involved in a sexual relationship with each other for eight years. So what did that mean?"

"Oh, I see where you're going with this," I told him. "I get it now," I said to pacify him. "It meant that we—"

"No, not *we*," he interrupted. "I want to know about *you*. What did it mean about *you*?"

I sat still, staring into Doug's eyes. I had told 95 percent of my story, but the 5 percent I hadn't told was where the lie lived. Doug didn't flinch. I let the 5 percent crawl deeper inside and called on my anger to protect me. I was afraid of being exposed.

"What did it mean?" I asked nearly in contempt. "I mean seriously, Doug. What do you think it meant?"

———

Melvin and Damon were my break-dance partners in the early 1980s. Mrs. Grdijan, completely ahead of her time, had set up a space behind our desks so that every day before language arts we could break-dance in the back of the room. Damon and I were better than Melvin, but Melvin's self-confidence (along with his Michael Jackson jacket) had people believing he was better than he actually was. Plus he had a "curl." Glistening soft black waves bounced around on his head while he broke. In breaking world, a mullet wasn't nearly as impressive as a Carefree Curl, and I knew it.

I didn't know Derek Daniels at the time, but rumor had it he could do the windmill, so he was like a celebrity to me. Actually he was like a celebrity to everyone. Once, at a school dance, he brought along his older cousin, who was dressed as Michael Jackson. All the students were delirious, as if his cousin really *was* Michael Jackson. However, I could see acne on his forehead and knew he was a phony. But if Derek had gotten down on the floor at the school dance and done the windmill, I would have screamed like a little girl at a One Direction concert.

In ninth grade, Derek and I became friends. After that, I found out firsthand that he actually could do the windmill. He tried to teach me one day after school, but it wasn't in the cards. And when I couldn't get my legs to stay in the air, he started calling me Cricket.

"I can't do it, man. I'm never gonna be able to do this," I told him.

"Hold it together, Cricket. Remember, it's for the people. It's for the people," he said as if I would be appointed class president the second I pulled this thing off.

I wasn't really a fan of being called Cricket, but I got used to it. Plus, Derek Daniels had given me a nickname, which was no small thing.

Derek liked girls and they liked him back. They seemed to like me only when I was hanging out with Derek. There was a girl in our neighborhood who had gotten really beautiful over summer break. She looked just like one of the women on *Knots Landing*. Derek said he would talk to her for me and that I should come to her house after school—that he'd meet me there. When I got to the end of her driveway, I took a deep breath.

Hold it together, Cricket.

I was convinced that being with Tina Johnson was a win for everyone. But not surprisingly, Tina Johnson was interested in Derek, which I completely understood since my mullet wasn't even in full bloom.

Break dancing, mullets, and my old nickname came and went. These things fall away from us and are never heard from again until we see a ridiculous old picture reminding us that it happened. But the hell we live through is another thing. We don't see pictures of ourselves being abused, miscarrying babies, battling cancer, or witnessing the atrocities of war. Those cruelties aren't stuck into old photo albums for us to thumb through. Instead they are emblazoned on the walls of our hearts like stubborn wallpaper that won't budge. We've done our best to take it down, but without the appropriate tools, we've left a mess behind. So we cover it back over with several more layers, doing what we can to spruce things up. But it's still under there, even if we're the only ones who know it.

Healing has no map; every person's experience is different. But if your journey is going to be successful, expect at some point to end up back at the scene of the crime, staring at the wreckage. People will tell you to move on, and they are partly right. But if you have tried and can't seem to, you must go back and see what happened with new eyes. And then you must tell your story without trying to make it palatable—for anyone. You have to tell the truth—the whole truth—expecting the painful passages to come when you do. If it gets to be too much, take a break. Dog-ear the page and return to it when you're good and ready, but plan to finish the book, because there's a beautiful ending to it.

I want to take a moment to encourage you about something. So often there is one thing holding us back from telling our stories: loyalty. Parents struggle to join their children in the fight for the truth because it is too painful for them to hear what happened on their watch. They agonize over what they did wrong, allowed to happen, didn't address, or covered up. But what they might not realize is that their sons and daughters have been carrying wounds, some for fifty or sixty years, and are losing their marriages, drinking themselves to death, abusing prescription drugs, road raging, or becoming addicted to porn, food, shopping, or control because the secrets and lies have been left unaddressed.

It would be too painful for my family if I told the truth, we've told ourselves, though not nearly as painful as holding it in all these years. We must never let another person's protection come before our own journey toward healing. God is in charge of protecting them, not us.

Anne Lamott says, "You own everything that happened to you. Tell your stories … If people wanted you to write warmly about them, they should've behaved better."[1] Living our lives to protect others is a burden we ought not to carry. It increases our shame, blurs reality, and will cause us to stumble through life without the sure footing we need to take ourselves up the mountain.

You don't have to name names, and you might want to consider whether telling your story to certain family members will bring injury or insult upon yourself. If it could, tell a therapist or close friend instead.

Telling our stories is how we authenticate who we really are. When we deny them and keep the lies hidden away, lies we've been asked or expected to keep, we find ourselves living someone else's story. And living someone else's story is like putting on their underwear: it's foul. Not only do you have their stink on you but you carry a toxic shame that will cripple your effectiveness as a child of God.

I've often heard people say, "I don't really have a story," but I've never found this to be true. Maybe you've had a feeling something wasn't right in your family of origin but could never put your finger on it because it wasn't as blatant as sexual or physical abuse. Trust your gut. Where there's pain, there's a wound.

When we live inside a lie for years, that lie becomes our reality. It might take some time to unravel things—to dig things up and find the truth. Or maybe it feels as if this thing is over, so why dredge it back up? After all, it's not as though the images are even clear anymore; they're fuzzy at best. Listen, you need to know that what's on the other side of that window has the power to dismember your life as you know it. And if you doubt what happened, wondering if it really mattered, let the pain be your litmus test. Where pain is present, a wound exists.

———————

Last night I attended the concert of a very popular worship leader named Matt Redman. With his pen, he has written some of the most beautifully contrasting song lyrics I've ever heard. You can feel the intensity of the backstory in his lyrics:

> *Blessed be your name*
> *When the sun's shining down on me*
> *When the world's all as it should be....*
>
> *Blessed be your name*
> *On the road marked with suffering*
> *Though there's pain in the offering.*[2]

Two-thirds of the way into the concert, everyone in the room sang out those words at the top of their lungs. Shortly thereafter, he began telling us his story. With great courage, he reached his hand back in time to grab hold of his past. As he dragged his past right into the present, we all watched his backstory become his storytold.

He said he knew what it was like to hurt. He said he had written those contrasting lyrics, which ebbed and flowed from joy to pain, because his wife had suffered four miscarriages. And then he said his dad had taken his own life while Matt was still just a boy and that at seven years old a predator sexually abused him.

All of that music and all of those lights, but when Matt Redman told his story, this was the moment heaven flooded the place with light, leaving us with almost no place to hide. According to statistics, in a crowd of nearly twelve hundred people, Matt Redman told between two and three hundred of us that we were not alone. His story did a swan dive right into our hearts and promised us hope. He had shown us what it looked like to tell the whole truth.

We have often said, "I want to make a difference, but with my broken past, what do I really have to offer?" Our stories are our offering. Talent wears out. Musicians' fingers will get gnarled in their old age and they will struggle to play their instrument like they used to. Younger generations will run off ahead of us in the business world. Beauty will fade and our professional influence will dwindle the older we get. But when all is said and done, we will still have our stories—stories that could change the world.

But do we know them? Do we understand them?

And will we tell them?

There is nothing more beautiful than a spotted-up old lady with suitcase skin and gumballed knuckles telling her story of redemption to those who need to know they can make something of themselves despite the terror that still lives in their hearts. In his book *Abba's*

Child, Brennan Manning says, "In a futile attempt to erase our past, we deprive the community of our healing gift. If we conceal our wounds out of fear and shame, our inner darkness can neither be illuminated nor become a light for others."[3]

Wounds need air. If something is kept covered by a bandage too long, it doesn't get better; it gets infected, and that infection can become toxic. The wounds on our souls also need air. Vulnerability, *saying* what happened, means ripping the bandage off so our stories can breathe.

I had a friend once tell me that if she's in the middle of a story and the plot gets chaotic or sad, she flips to the end of the book to see if it ends well. If it does, she continues reading. If it doesn't, she tosses the book aside and finds a story that does end well.

Our lives are stories, but there are no prewritten endings to which we can flip and then decide if we'll keep reading. Some of our loved ones and friends bow out of our stories because they'd like to be spared the pain of what they are sure will be a bad ending. But as Clint Eastwood once said, "Every story has its demands."[4]

The story of the Son of God was a bit complicated, wasn't it? And then he died. But if we stick around, sometimes the worst stories end up being the most powerful. Because out of nowhere we'll come across an epilogue with a twist that will make all that death somehow worth it—perhaps a resurrection.

When Doug asked me, "What did [the incest] mean about *you*?" I couldn't answer the question because at the time, I simply wasn't ready. So instead, for the next several years, I searched for the answer to that question as well as many others.

Confessions were made along the way, which were humiliating and painful and then completely liberating. But once I discovered that lies are powerful only in the dark, I dragged every one I could find into the light so Jesus could get his beautiful hands on them. And for the first time in my life, the lies became manageable. Curable? Not completely, but definitely manageable.

Doug sat across from me week after week and watched as thirty years of pent-up shame blasted my face with tears. It was so terribly painful—so wonderfully freeing.

Initially I didn't want a journey; I wanted only an arrival. But the dusty roads, wrong turns, flat tires, and angels in disguise were an imperative part of that arrival because they showed me where I had come from rather than simply where I was. And in order to be useful, I needed to know where I had been.

Maybe you feel you've already dealt with your past but are now beginning to sense a twisting in your spirit. That clutch on your heart may be God trying to tell you something; that perhaps there is still something back there—that *one thing* that needs to be unearthed from the dirt of your past.

You might feel that going back will break you, but maybe going back will make you instead. For me, it was undeniably painful before it was peaceful, but God was preparing me to tell my story. There were times I thought the sun might disappear altogether, but eventually I saw daybreak. And when I did, every secret, plot twist, and pitfall sneaked out to the end of my tongue, threw its arms wide open, and dove right into someone else's story, illuminating their darkness.

If God really is calling us out of our hiding places, he must believe we are stronger than we think we are. And maybe he's right. Maybe we just need to be brave.

"If we conceal our wounds out of fear and shame, our inner darkness can neither be illuminated nor become a light for others."

So hold it together, Cricket, because it's for the people.

Yes, it is.

So I hid myself away in the carpet of the earth and began telling my story. Soon the other crickets, grasshoppers, and caterpillars appeared to keep me company. They watched as I dipped a blade of grass into a puddle of rain and wrote hope-filled words, filling up leaf after leaf with the harsh and chaotic words of my life, transcribing my broken story that had never been told. But it wasn't enough to write it; I had to say it.

I cleared my throat and read to them of sexual abuse and parental poverty, of neglect, self-loathing, and fear. They sat before me listening closely as I read page after page. When the panic and terror seized me and I could no longer speak, they cried out on my behalf. They prayed for me. "Hold it together, Cricket. It's for the people."

I turned over every stone I could find, exposing all the places my shame had been hidden. Darkness was driven from the forest floor, and eventually their eyes were opened.

Realizing they too had stories, they began sharing them with one another. They rubbed their legs together and sang songs of terror, abuse, hostility, loneliness, genocide, and suffering. But after some time, their melodies began turning into songs of deliverance, healing, love, and redemption. They wrote the songs that made the whole world sing and were grateful someone cared enough to listen.

And after knowing all there was to know, not a secret between us, they wrapped themselves up in cocoons and turned themselves into butterflies to say thank you. They were all invited into "the family way" with a story and a song of their own—a song we all sang. Together.

PART 4

REDEMPTION 2.0

REDEEMED 2.0
God's Love Is Not Appropriate

*Redemption needs finagling, not because we are inclined
to make sure it is happening even when it isn't but
because we have misunderstood it. We have believed
that redemption is possible only minus a death. We're
okay that Jesus had to die for his redemptive story, but
personally we're not looking to get into all that. There is
no redemption in death, we think. But we are wrong.*

I wrapped up my duties at church one Sunday and drove to see my sister. I'd led three worship songs that weekend, all of which could have been used for a funeral. One lyric really got to me: "I want to be close, close to your side. So heaven is real and death is a lie."[1] I pulled the microphone away from my mouth every time those words came. I couldn't bear to sing them out loud, so I let the congregation sing them for me. I figured maybe *they* believed them.

I met my family at Maude Neiding Park in Amherst, Ohio, where Trina's granddaughter Lana was having her sixth birthday party. Just before heading into the parking lot, I pulled my car over and stashed a fresh pack of smokes in the glove box in case my mom was there. I smoke less than one cigarette per year. There's not much to hide, but I don't want to ruin the image I've got going with her: more Charlie Brown, less Charlie Sheen.

My goal in visiting Trina was to clear the stress from her life as much as possible. She has always been the glue in her family and often comes off as though she's indestructible. She's a make-it-happen, never-overwhelmed, always-there kind of girl. But when cancer arrived, it quickly became the antagonist in her story. All its minions were hard at work, complicating her care, relationships, finances, and everyday life stresses. She needed to find a new normal that didn't include *being* the glue, but being glued herself.

The party was over shortly after I arrived, so we packed up and headed for Trina's place.

"We want to get married," she told me, sitting on the couch in her new apartment. She and Chuck sat side by side, squeezed tightly together.

"And we're wondering if you could help us out with that," he said, rubbing her arm. I had seen her battle cancer five years ago with a man who didn't have it in him to be there for her—to put her first. But this was different: different home, different man, different love.

My main concern was her well-being. I didn't want to marry them if it would in any way compromise her care, especially since her ex had excellent insurance that would continue covering Trina unless she remarried. But I was also thinking about Chuck's future—that if his insurance was not what it needed to be, Trina's enormous medical bills could swamp him with a debt he'd never be able to pay off. But I could see their love. They were already married as far as I was concerned. A part of me wanted to say, "Let's just do it right now, here in this little apartment. You guys are already married in God's eyes anyway. Let's just say your vows and call it a day."

That night I slept on the couch with their Boston terrier, Lulu, huddled up next to me. Amid the sadness of Trina's cancer, there was great relief in knowing that Chuck was with her. I can't tell you how good it felt watching him walk into the bedroom with her—that she was not alone.

When I woke up the next morning, my intention was to get Trina's mind off her cancer and enjoy the day. The two of us picked up our mom and headed to a local hole-in-the-wall diner for breakfast. We drank coffee, ate pancakes, and felt like family. Our conversation was as uninteresting and as normal as any other day, which felt good.

Mom told us she was having a tooth pulled because one of her crowns had broken. When we realized she wasn't planning to put anything in its place, we laid the smackdown because we have this thing about teeth.

"You're not planning to pull the tooth and leave a hole, are you?"

"You won't be able to see it, Son. It's way back here," she told us, sticking a finger in her mouth and pulling back on her cheek.

"Mom, no," was all Trina said. It wasn't up for debate. To Trina, pulling a tooth without filling the hole was a mortal sin and she was trying to save her mother's soul.

"Do you know how much it will cost to replace the tooth with an implant?" Mom asked.

"You're too pretty, Mom," I said, playing on her feminine wiles.

"Well then, okay, I guess. If you both think it's the right thing to do."

"Without question," I affirmed.

Apparently a cord of *two* strands is also not easily broken. We had just prevented bad stuff from happening. We couldn't cure cancer, but we could definitely bully Mom into putting her teeth back the way God intended.

On the ride home, we made a pit stop at Drug Mart. Mom wasn't looking too good in the backseat and said she needed to use the bathroom. I pulled the car as close to the entrance as I could, and Mom darted out without even shutting the door. Ten minutes later, when she got back in the car, she looked relieved. "That was a close one, Matthew." Trina let out a giggle from the passenger seat, and the three of us laughed ourselves to tears all the way home.

Yes, there were good days, and thank God for them. We needed them. But the mood quickly changed as soon as Trina and I headed back to her apartment.

"How could this happen to me? It's so not fair," she told me. "I finally have a man who treats me so good—I'm happy!" she said with frustration in her eyes. "And now this?"

"I'm so sorry, Wee. You're right," I said in agreement. "It's *not* fair."

"I can't even get married because of this stupid insurance," she said, wiping tears from her cheeks.

My heart was broken for her, and before I knew it I blurted out, "Says who? I mean, seriously, why can't you get married?"

"Because of the insurance, Matt, and because of what it could do to Chuck. It could totally wipe him out financially, and I don't want him left behind with all my medical bills."

"So let's think outside the box for a minute." I spend much of my professional time scouring the Internet and keeping an ear to the ground for great ideas. Now I had one. "Let's just do it," I told her.

"We can't. How could we?" she asked.

"Well, I *am* a pastor," I reminded her. "Who cares about court records? You love him and he loves you. You're already married in God's eyes. Let's do it. I'll marry you guys. We'll have a ceremony, exchange vows—why not?"

She was quiet, staring off into space, perhaps seeing herself as Chuck's wife. I knew it was what she wanted. And then, breaking the silence, she asked as if she were a little girl, "You think we really could?"

"I *know* we could," I affirmed. "If this is what you want, we'll make it happen. And it will be beautiful."

"I want his last name," she told me.

"Then have it. It won't be on your checks or driver's license, but who cares? Change your Facebook, use it in every single letter you write—it doesn't matter."

"I wouldn't want anyone to know it wasn't legal."

"Who would know? Just tell people you are getting married; they'll assume the rest. This is about spirit and love, not binding documents and shared taxes. He's your man—I know that, and so do you."

It was no time to be conventional. Her life was hanging in the balance, and I believed to my core that this girl who had suffered such great pain in her childhood, who had never made "partner" in her own legalized marriage of twenty-nine years, deserved to exchange vows and promise her love and devotion to the only man who had ever really loved her the way she needed to be loved.

"Well," she said, drying the rest of the tears on her face, "let's talk to him when he gets home from work. But where would we do it?"

"How about Hilton Head?" Heather and I had already planned a vacation in Hilton Head over the Fourth of July. It only made sense. "We could do it on the beach."

She smiled, seeing it all in her head. "Okay," she said almost in a whisper. She deserved to take Big New Beautiful Boyfriend as her husband and for him to take her—to have her and to hold her, in sickness and in health, for as long as they both shall live.

God works in mysterious ways, we tell ourselves. And as long as we're okay with what that looks like, as long as the mystery doesn't go beyond what we believe to be sensible, we'll give ourselves over to the idea that God might concoct something original and unique that we never saw coming. But most of the time, we need for that mystery to make sense. We need for it to be appropriated in a way that is accessible to our understanding. We need to make sure it doesn't butt up against our theology or ideology in a way that makes God look foolish—so *we* don't look foolish. But if we can get over ourselves and our rules, if we can finally give in to the mystery, there's no telling what God will do.

> Have you ever come on anything quite like this
> extravagant generosity of God, this deep, deep wis-
> dom? It's way over our heads. We'll never figure it
> out. (Rom. 11:33 THE MESSAGE)

When Chuck got home from work, we broke the news and all he said was, "I don't need a piece of paper to tell me who my wife is." And that was that. We were planning a holy unsanctioned wedding.

We were high on love and had just started in about the wedding dress when Trina got a phone call. If the world were less cruel, the call would have been from a wedding planner, but it wasn't: it was from a doctor.

"Your bone scan is back, Trina," I heard the doctor say.

"Oh," was all she said. She had told me the day before that the results of the bone scan didn't matter.

"Of course they matter," I told her.

"No, they don't," she said, as if this were all just a series of inconveniences we needed to settle down about.

I listened intently while sitting next to her.

"The results are positive for more cancer." Her blue eyes stared straight ahead and she let out the quietest sigh. It mattered.

Chuck sat on the other side of her, watching her face. Trina told me he had cried out to God in prayer the night before, weeping and begging for her life—for her healing. He had never been a man of prayer, but all that was changing. The woman he so desperately loved needed a miracle to remain in this world. He was all in. "Where have you been all my life?" he said to her every morning as they woke up. Or she'd wake up to find him staring at her with a smile on his face.

She teased him about being a stalker, but he would gently reply, "You just make me so happy. I love watching you sleep."

"The cancer is now in your pelvis, sternum, lower back, and scapula." My heart raced. I couldn't bear more bad news. I sat next to her in silence, angered by what seemed to be God's will.

God, tell me why. The cancer is everywhere! But where are you?

"This doesn't change treatment. It just means we need to add a medication to the chemotherapy that will strengthen your bones."

"Okay," was all she said.

"Do you have any questions for me today?" I restrained myself from grabbing the phone out of her hand.

"No."

"Okay, Trina, then we will still see you on the tenth of June."

Show me a hero and I'll write you a tragedy.
—F. Scott Fitzgerald, "Notebook E"

———————

After driving thirteen and a half hours through the beautiful green mountains of Tennessee and North Carolina, we arrived in Hilton Head. It had rained most of the trip, but every so often things would dry up and the clouds would stretch across the mountains, drinking up the earth's water. Evalee snapped pictures out the window with her iPod and Chloe begged us to stop for more food.

Trina and Chuck had arrived several days earlier, so as we pulled in with a minivan full of empty cups, candy wrappers, blankets, power cables, books, and the last shred of patience left in us, they greeted us in the driveway like an old married couple. Trina's eyes were puffy from crying.

"She's having a hard time with her hair falling out," Chuck told me as I brought in the luggage.

"Where is she now?" I asked. It wasn't like her to disappear the moment we arrived.

"In the bathroom throwing up the salad she ate for dinner." Although it hadn't even been made yet, he was already living out his "in sickness and in health" wedding vow.

Trina wore bandanas around the house to protect what was left of her hair for the wedding. Her eyebrows were penciled in and most of her eyelashes were gone. Her abdomen was swollen from the chemo and steroids. Several times that evening, Heather told her how pretty she looked, and she did, but I could see the wear and tear of the cancer.

Like a big sister, she still managed to boss us around, telling us what rooms we were staying in and showing the girls how to use the microwave. She was still here, still fighting, still Trina.

"You should have the wedding tomorrow," Heather told her, "on July Fourth. It's Independence Day, so it only makes sense."

But she wanted her own day. "I'd rather do it on the fifth," she told us.

"Then the fifth it is!"

The next day we made preparations for the wedding, and while the girls shopped for a wedding dress, Chuck and I went for a ride in a 1989 Porsche Carrera convertible a friend had lent us for the week. Winding through South Carolina roads under a canopy of trees with the top down was a brief emancipation from cancer we both needed.

I thought we just might find a local tattoo parlor and add a new one to his collection: "Born to Ride."

Chuck was a grace I couldn't begin to explain, even though contrary to everything we'd been brought up to believe, he and my sister were living in sin. Be that as it may, their love for each other was undeniable.

Sometimes God uses what is so much grittier than we've ever thought appropriate. But God is not appropriate when it comes to love. He doesn't ration it out, giving us just enough to keep us from starving. It might feel like that for a time, but then for reasons we never understand he pours it out lavishly. And if we know what's good for us, we'll accept the love he provides even if it seems inappropriate by all we thought we knew.

The wedding day was lazy, the kind of day you relish on vacation. We had coffee in the morning while Chloe and Evalee drove the golf cart around the neighborhood. Trina decided against getting married on the beach because of how beautifully the South Carolina trees framed the back of our vacation home.

I don't know that any of us remember when the wedding got started because we took our time that day. There was no rush. It was all we had come for.

As the ceremony began, Chuck and I stood on the back porch dwarfed by giant crooked Southern trees filled with Spanish moss. It was the most beautiful scene, like heaven on earth. Heather played music from her laptop while the girls filed out the door in white dresses and with grins on their faces.

And then we saw her. She looked twenty-three. It was the day she'd always hoped for, the day she'd never had. Our hearts leapt with faith, hope, and love as she walked down our makeshift aisle. Roses lined the way as Norah Jones sang, "My heart is drenched in wine, but you'll be on my mind forever."[2]

They didn't wait for me to say, "You may now kiss the bride," because this moment wasn't about propriety or following a script. They kissed each other all throughout the ceremony. They were in love; it was all that mattered.

Both of them said "I do" with tears in their eyes, and just like that, Big New Beautiful Boyfriend became Big New Beautiful Husband. And for the first time in her life, Trina felt loved—*truly* loved—by a man.

Her core father wound had sent her searching nearly a lifetime for the kind of unconditional love this day had brought her. And I find it beautiful and even a bit haunting that Big New Beautiful Husband's name just happens to be "Charles Edward," the exact same name as our biological father's.

I wrote down his name with Becky's pen and put it in my jar.

Cancer was not the word of the hour that day; *love* was. It didn't matter how inappropriately it had arrived on the scene, because on that day, love was winning. Finally. It was winning.

Researcher and storyteller Brené Brown says, "The people who have a strong sense of love and belonging believe they are worthy of love and belonging."[2] She goes on to say that "whole-hearted people" are those who have the courage to tell their stories with their whole heart. But in order to tell your story, you must know your story.

If we see ourselves as worthy, we have most likely been acquainted with unworthiness. In order to inspire hope, we must have at some point in our lives been hopeless. And we can only be redeemed when we know what it is to be condemned. We cannot be saved from something we don't suppose we are suffering from. This is what it means to know your story—to know your pain and loss to their fullest potential for evil in your life's bloodline. Because when true redemption goes searching to make things right, it will be looking not among those who *don't* need a doctor, but among those who are hanging on the gallows, gasping their final breaths alongside the unredeemed.

Several years ago I had a vision. It is the only vision I've ever had.

There was a prayer experience at my church, and as part of that experience, several rooms were decorated with different themes. The very last room was the "Son Room," representing the story of the prodigal son. A large oblong dinner table sat in the middle of the room. Someone had set it for a celebration. There were beautiful plates, crystal glasses, and embroidered linens because, as the story goes, a son was lost but had been found.

Chairs were lined up around the perimeter of the wall so those who entered the room could sit and reflect on this scene. I opted to sit at the table. To this day I don't know why I placed myself directly in the story, but I did.

I sat one seat from the head of the table because I had already pictured Jesus occupying that seat. I picked up a floral china plate and flipped it over: "Noritake." *Wow*, I thought. *Someone spared no expense.* The red carpet had been rolled out. I sat quietly, eyeballing my upside-down reflection in the bend of a silver teapot, and that's when my vision began.

As I looked around the table, the empty seats began filling up with members of the family I was born into: first my mom and Trina, then Tim, and finally my biological father, Charles Edward. My parents were divorced before I was three years old, so this was the first time I had ever seen my splintered family together.

We were gathered around this beautiful table where each of us had our own seat. My dad was sitting next to my mom, and although they had been divorced for almost forty years, in this scene neither one of them knew anything of broken wedding vows or broken homes. He was talking softly to her and looking her straight in the eye. He leaned over and kissed her on the cheek, and she smiled sweetly back at him. They were together. They were happy.

Tim, who had been gone for almost twenty years, sat across the table from them. He was watching them. And as he did, the part of him that was so broken in this life was being made whole.

Trina was next to Tim, and I was next to her. She and I were talking and laughing like we always had.

There we sat: the five of us plus one. Jesus was sitting at the head of the table now, and his eye was on us. It had always been on us.

We didn't say grace before we ate because this meal was a grace in itself.

We ate and filled our bellies with redemption, knowing we were there at love's invitation. We had been welcomed to the way things should have been, to the way things one day would be, and, in this beautiful moment, to the way things were.

A vision is not always a reality for us here on earth, that's the sad part. But once we understand we are worthy of love and belonging, that's when we'll find God in the ruins. That's when we'll give God access to the broken places within us. And that's when we can begin again.

> Then He who sat on the throne [at the head of
> the table] said, "Behold, I make all things new."
> (Rev. 21:5 NKJV)

BROTHELS AND BASEMENTS
A Compassionate God

The worst part of our suffering isn't the suffering itself; it's the wondering whether or not we will find ourselves after the dust has settled.

Keegan's blond hair is nearly white, which makes him easy to spot, and I often make my way across our church's atrium to see how he is doing.

"So tell me what's new, Keegan," I always say, starting things up. I love this kid, and in the way that he is able, I suppose he loves me back.

By the age of two, Keegan had already been through the wringer and experienced more pain than some people experience over their entire lives. With a backstory like his, one of the challenges he faces is connecting with those he loves at a deeper level. His birth parents had low IQs and abused drugs, which affected his capacity to attach to others. The small connection he has with me is most likely due to the fact that we are not very close, seeing each other only at church.

He always engages me, telling me something new about himself, most recently filling me in on the sordid details of a book his sister was writing that I have been written into.

"She put you in jail," he says, laughing, and goes on to tell me that I would be seeing my family only through bulletproof glass. But each time this ten-year-old boy talks, I struggle to listen because I think about all the pain he has seen in his short life and wonder if his spirit will ever be able to overcome it. Inside myself, I am pulling for him.

Last weekend I saw Keegan in the basement of our church, hanging out with his adoptive family of seven. His dad was giving the message that weekend on the topic of family, and Keegan had participated in the preaching portion of that service although he had never said a word on the platform. His dad acknowledged him and each one of his brothers and sisters, informing our church body about their distinct personality traits and how each one of those magical characteristics contributed to the family unit. Keegan was "the clown." He made them all laugh and always had.

Afterward I felt compelled to affirm Keegan, so I sat down next to him and said, "Hey, man, that was like the first message you've ever preached in church."

"Yep," he responded in agreement even though his dad had done all the talking. He didn't laugh and he didn't brush me off. He simply nodded as if this had been one of many sermons he would eventually give.

"Were you nervous up there? There were like two thousand people staring at you."

"Not really." He was nonchalant about the whole thing.

Maybe twice in a decade would you ever hear me say that God has laid something on my heart. I am mostly guided by his hand rather than instructed by his words. So when I hear his voice within me, I flip the switch to autopilot because I don't want to get in the way.

"Keegan," I said and turned my chair toward his so he would be looking me in the eyes, "maybe this is something you'll end up doing." His dark brown eyes stared straight at me. "Maybe one day you'll give messages to people and tell them about Jesus." He nodded again as though it might be a possibility—as though he would give it some thought. "I could see you doing it," I told him. And I could.

Keegan had plans to drive a truck one day and had even practiced his driving from the passenger seat of the family camper while on a three-month road trip out west. Overhearing our little chat, his mom threw in her two cents. "Maybe you could be bi-vocational, Keegan. Maybe you could split your time between driving a truck during the week and preaching on the weekends."

Driving a truck and preaching are not the typical dreams a mother has for her kids, but I wonder if Keegan's parents are holding out hope that his life will be "just okay" and that "just okay" might actually be of great relief to them, considering the difficulties that undoubtedly lie ahead.

I'll bet deep down inside they're hoping he'll discover something he loves to do rather than find himself on the broken path so many kids with a backstory like his seem to find. But there comes a time we must be reasonable with life, especially when it has been so unreasonable with us. We have to lower our expectations and swap our dreams for reality. And to be honest, driving a truck might keep him out of trouble when it's time. But something in me— blind, stupid hope, the desire to see something broken get fixed, or the voice that speaks to me only twice a decade—felt that Keegan would preach one day and that preaching God's love to others just might be his redemption.

Poet Sherman Alexie once wrote, "What you pawn I will redeem."[1] Amen. So be it.

Ultimately all the unredeemed really want to know is that they are capable of being redeemed in *some* way—that even if they have been pawned off by random life circumstances (their family of origin, past mistakes, simple human nature), they still have it in them to morph into something beautiful and useful.

Regarding Keegan, it's easy for us to think, *Wow, this kid got a new family who really loves him. His story has already been rewritten. He has a chance in life.* But we cannot forget that being redeemed is painful—that receiving the love that is supposed to replace the neglect or abuse is often agonizing, like nails down a chalkboard. Before Keegan got his new family, his default settings for giving and receiving love were short-circuited. So if our expectation is that Keegan will one day be capable of receiving love without wincing, we might have deeply underestimated the power of our wounds.

The opening lyrics to the Matt Maher song "Empty and Beautiful" say this:

> *My past won't stop haunting me.*
> *In this prison there's a fight between*
> *who I am and who I used to be.*[2]

The first time I heard these words, I thought of a hundred things in my past I didn't believe I could ever write about—things I was certain made God cringe and the heavens go silent while a communion of saints stopped what they were doing to whisper a prayer on my behalf.

But then I remember the words of civil rights activist Audre Lorde, "Wherever the bird with no feet flew, she found trees with no limbs,"[3] and I'm reminded that this broken bird will always have a place to land.

When I was Keegan's age, I already had a sex life. Other kids my age weren't eyeballing each other sexually in elementary school, but I was. My default settings had been quashed in the basement of my own home, and while I should have been thinking about kickball, art class, or how cute Megan Fields was, I was thinking about nudity—in particular, naked boys.

I came of age in a basement—the same place where so many broken things had happened with my brother. That basement was the enemy's pawnshop, and God, it seemed, was just another loan shark. The enemy had gambled away my soul until there was nothing left of it. And when it came time to pay for all the racketeering, it appeared as if God hadn't done a thing but had pardoned his debt altogether. That's why I shut God out in the first place; I could no longer stand the hypocrisy. So until I could get a better grasp on his plan or, more accurately, his chaos, I had to let him go.

"If you go down this road," the religious will tell you, "just be careful. Don't go too far or you'll end up losing your faith." But the fear of losing our faith is not a good enough reason for having it in the first place. At some point, if we are ever to forgive God and move on *with* him, we must ask him about his poor guardianship, we must give ourselves permission to cross-examine his weak defense.

In some ways it is devastating to tell God all you wish he had done differently, saved you from, or converted you into. But when the God of your church of origin gives you the same remedial cliché for your pain time and time again, there's not a thing wrong with sticking your middle finger right in his face. You might think this kind of bad spiritual behavior will cause you to lose your faith altogether—that you'll end up losing sight of God. But maybe the moment you flip God the bird is the exact moment he looks into your eyes and says, "Well done, my good and faithful servant."

Most of us would agree that King David, whose claim to fame is being a man after God's own heart, took on an accusatory tone in Psalm 44, when he said,

> But now you've walked off and left us,
>> you've disgraced us and won't fight for us.
> You made us turn tail and run;
>> those who hate us have cleaned us out.
> You delivered us as sheep to the butcher,
>> you scattered us to the four winds.
> You sold your people at a discount—
>> you made nothing on the sale.
>
> You made people on the street,
>> urchins, poke fun and call us names.
> You made us a joke among the godless,
>> a cheap joke among the rabble.
> Every day I'm up against it,
>> my nose rubbed in my shame—

Gossip and ridicule fill the air,

people out to get me crowd the street.

(vv. 9–16 THE MESSAGE)

Knowing I wasn't the only one who thought ill of God provided the kind of safe company that put me at ease.

Safe company. Man, do we need it.

Remember Robert and Ann, the couple in our young married group back in 1994 (see chapter 3)? After having told me about Robert's duplicitous lifestyle and the downward spiral of their marriage, Ann had also said, "Our church was not ready for the U-Haul of baggage we were dragging behind us." Sadly, I understood her words completely. For years I had longed for the church to be a safe place where I could reexamine my faith with fear and trembling and anger. I needed it to be a place where I could ask the tough questions—where I could expose God's short sale on my life, on Robert's life, on Keegan's life, on yours. But the church wasn't the place I hoped it would be.

I'm guessing my church would have given me six months to work things out rather than the six years it would take, and I'm not sure they would have been wrong to hold those expectations of me. After all, I was a pastor.

But if not within the loving arms of the church, then where? Why are God's people so much less resilient? And what are we afraid of?

Even though Robert had cheated on her, eventually Ann took him back into her home. He was not the man she believed him to be when they were first married, and his cruelties to her were

unimaginable. But the first time she heard about the enemy's cruelties to her broken-down husband (his being molested as a child), she
understood just how deep his wounds had gone—why he wasn't the
man she thought he was. And in that moment, she didn't believe he
was bad anymore, only broken.

"I'm done talking about it for right now," she said while sitting
at Chipotle in Lexington, Kentucky. "Sometimes it just gets a little
too hard to hear."

I couldn't imagine the hurt she'd been through, but her face
was filled with grace while she spoke, as if the pain was now riding
shotgun. It wouldn't be leaving her anytime soon, maybe never, but
it was no longer in the driver's seat of her life.

"I'm so sorry," he said, squeezing her hand for all he'd done. This
was no longer a ruse. He meant it. Robert had been converted. And
when he had, Ann removed the chain from the door and let him
come back home.

God watches us squirm. I don't know if I will ever get used to it.
I think of the atrocities of this world, such as ten-year-old Indian
girls being sexually violated time and time again in the brothels of
Mumbai, and I know God sees it happen, but also that he doesn't
intervene in the way that I would—that any of us would. When
I sent God away, I wanted to know what was happening in the
heavenly realms when life was brutalizing his children. I pictured
God in Indian brothels, staring on. I imagined him leaning against
the laundry machine in my basement, seeing all of it. In brothels

and basements, I knew he was there. But what was he doing if not intervening?

While writing this book, I sent an earlier portion of the manuscript to a good friend of mine. In chapter 5, I had written this statement: "He participated in their horrors by being present."

This is what my friend sent back to me: "Where is God? He is hanging there on the gallows. He's not just in the brothel with the girl being violated; he IS being violated."

He IS being violated.

I let the thought sink in, and for the first time in my life the crucified God looked different to me. He wasn't watching; he was receiving. Before this moment, I had compassion for God only on the Friday he was executed. That was the day *his* human rights were violated. But now I was faced with the idea of his crucifixion being stretched out until the end of time—that in every abysmal crime against us, every suicide, every abuse, every murder, rape, and addiction, God himself was being violated.

God wasn't staring on in the brothels of Mumbai; he was stuck on a dirty floor with a pedophile on top of him. And he wasn't leaning against the laundry machine in my basement; he was being pierced, crushed, bruised, and wounded so eventually *I* could be healed. It happened to him every time it happened to me. It was him, the same as it was me.

Was it possible that God needed my compassion? Was it true that all of our suffering combined was the total weight of God's suffering?

Is this what is meant by the *weight of glory*?

If we were abused, then so was he. If we were orphaned, then he was too. All of a sudden I wanted to reach out to God—to take care of him. He had been broken and abused the same as I, the same as Keegan, the same as Robert—violated by his own family and left behind to suffer and die.

I no longer wanted him out in the cold. I wanted him back inside the warmth of my heart.

MELODY UNCHAINED
Finding Your Faith Again

I don't have a problem believing that God is proud
of me. And I imagine he loves to tell his friends
about me. This very specific sense of self feels like
an imprint—a song I've had nothing to do with.
I'm not burdened by it at all. Truth be told, it
gets me through. And for all that has happened
in my life, I suppose he knew I would need it.

There's an article circulating the Internet called "The God Molecule."[1] It's about an African tribe said to count the day of someone's existence as the moment his mother first thinks of him. And when the mother feels it is time to bring her child into the world, she goes off by herself and listens for the song that specifically belongs to her child, because every child has a song.

Once the mother hears her child's song, she teaches it to the father and they sing it together as they are making love to conceive the child. And then as the child is being born, the midwives sing the same song and it becomes the very first thing the child hears upon entering the world.

But the story continues.

The people of the village also know the child's song, and because they do, whenever a child comes to harm, perhaps falling down, someone in the village will pick him up and sing his song to comfort him. Or if a child does something wonderful, the song is sung to honor the person he is becoming. Conversely, if a child commits an offense against one of the other villagers or is caught in a social scandal, he is called to the center of the village and the people of the tribe gather around and sing his song to remind him who he *really* is—that he is not the offensive person he has become in his moment of depravity.

The child's song is forever connected to his identity and is sung all throughout his life. So when he comes to die, the last thing he will hear in the land of the living is his children and grandchildren standing around his bed and singing his song as he takes his final breath.

Even in death, his song remains. It goes with him into eternity to be sung by the saints who've gone on before him.

God also has a song. It is his identity, and it will not change.

Tragedy cannot change his melody, nor can heartache or disbelief. Even death of many kinds cannot alter the cadence, rhythm, or time signature of his song. It is not a pop song. It is not jazz or a spiritual. It is not a lament. It's an instrumental with a vocal cadenza that has the most surprising lyrics we've ever heard. We will never figure out the meter, rhyme scheme, or essence of those lyrics. And although we are never to stop trying to make sense of his unchained melody, sometimes it is better to simply listen to the music rather than inventory the melody and lyrics.

A part of us will always long to know the closing line—to wrap our hearts, minds, and souls around the answer to our pain or tragedy. But I'm more certain than ever that our search for answers, which has so often come up empty, is a reminder that there is another song out there that does not belong to nor identify us—a song bigger than ours that identifies God alone.

Often it seems that two-thirds of God's song is the sound track to tragedy and ruin. And because the math doesn't make sense to us, we either close up our hearts entirely or refuse to live in reality, hanging our theology on spiritual clichés. Or we write God off as a liar, a cheat, or even nonexistent, the biggest scam of all time. But if we learn to live with the tension of God's major *and* minor melody, we will find his beautiful refrain ringing out in our lives, which is his purpose for us—his calling from the core wound.

We are a part of God's song, but we are most certainly not all of it. Our thoughts and prayers are just one measure in the entirety of his symphony. And our life's pain, poured out in a series of minor chords, often fades before we get the chance to hear it resolve. We would give anything to hear our dissonant melodies settle into lighter passages, but we must trust that the master conductor hears it all—that he knows the cadence and rhythm of our song by heart.

But God is not just the master conductor. He is also the composer who is transcribing every musical notation with his pen—shaping each note in the space between our trials and triumphs. And in that space, the space between, all who choose to listen will hear his song. And we will never forget it.

If we decide to be part of the chorus, at some point we are going to need to accept that the immeasurable agony we've felt over the span of our lifetime was him. We've done everything we can to separate God from our pain—to place the responsibility on any other thing we can find—or else we would have to walk away from him.

God has not always caused our pain, but he has *always* allowed for it. That's the hard truth. Harder still is that we don't know why. We will never know what makes him God. We can make our guesses, but in the middle of our pain, the answers wouldn't matter anyway. We need *more* than answers. We need the love of God, no matter how awkward or fumbly.

God knows your name. And in the immense pain, he whispers it under his breath, sending it out as a love song—a melody of grace notes that in time will balance every dissonant chord of your life. He is the one who, at this very moment, wherever you may be, has hung an invisible banner over your head that reads,

> I have redeemed you; I have called you by name,
> you are mine. (Isa. 43:1 ESV)

Before I began this journey, I wasn't exactly sure where my questions would lead—to believing or unbelieving. I was ready for either. I wasn't overwhelmed at the thought of changing professions if that's where the path took me. The pain of simplistic and defective answers to life's most powerful and haunting questions had become far greater than the pain of putting God on trial, so I stepped out in faith, though many would have considered it stepping into *un*faith.

It seems silly now to expect that any true believer wouldn't have a steady stream of doubt and anger toward God on their faith journey. Even an atheist would expect this. So after years of giving myself permission to doubt God and be angry with him, I finally came to the end of myself. It was time to decide if I really believed.

I searched every inch of my pain to see if God was nearby, digging through the wreckage and ruins to see if he was buried somewhere in the debris. I quieted my heart in the peaceful moments, listening for the slightest clue to any real presence there. In the pain and in the peace, I felt something. *I* did. Sometimes it was so obvious to me, while other times it wasn't. But during many of these moments, the ones I had collected in my special jar, I found myself unable to deny a higher power. There was something out there—something greater than myself, something greater than humanity—and I could finally hear the music.

If I were to deny his presence, I would need another place for all these peculiar moments when I *had* sensed God—for all the things in my jar that kept pointing me to something bigger. Without God, I would have to *un*recognize his song in my mother's holy wail at my brother's funeral. Without God, I would need to believe that Becky's pen had no magic in it at all. Without God, I would need to believe that he never saw what was happening to me in the basement with my brother—that I really had been alone after all.

This "something greater" didn't look anything like what my church of origin had confirmed in me. My mom's image was certainly closer with her sensitive, gracious, and hopeful descriptions of Jesus. But in the end, something greater was wooing me as I stood before the corn in Westfield. And in my recovery, something greater had given me the capacity to be healed from the abuses of this world—healing that wasn't academic but that drifted into me as the tears flowed out of me. God, in his own way, was my something greater.

There comes a point in our lives when either we will believe in a higher power or we won't. I don't have a desire to convince you of a higher power for my sake, as though your faith might ramp up my own. It is simply a question we all must answer for ourselves: *Is there more?*

If we experience love, hope, and joy, where do those moments come from? Are they just coincidence? Are they simply neurons transmitting impulses within our brains? Or is something greater singing its song into our lives? And in the moments when our hearts are broken in two, when we see towers fall to the ground on our TV screens, when we are stuck in our childhood bedroom with an uncle whose violation of us will stretch all throughout our lives, are we really alone?

"If I wasn't alone, then why didn't you intervene?"

This is the question I asked God straight to his face—and it was a perfectly reasonable thing to ask. If he had answered with only "Because" or "I'm sorry," I would have thought he was no better than me, because that's what *I* would've said. But he never answered my questions at all, most likely because answers were not what I needed. But if answers couldn't convince me of God, what could?

As kids, Trina and I spent hours in her room listening to vinyl records on a red, white, and blue record player. Because the record player belonged to her, I was at the mercy of her musical tastes. We listened to Andy Gibb, Foreigner, Leif Garrett, Randy Newman, Journey, Gloria Gaynor, Elvis Presley, and Barry Manilow.

I didn't know a thing about music at the time, but in fourth grade, at her prompting, I signed up for the school talent show. She took me to Camelot Music at Midway Mall to pick out a song, which was the easiest part. I chose the song I had most requested in her bedroom: "Can't Smile Without You," by Barry Manilow.

Over the weeks leading up to the talent show, I listened to that song a hundred times, committing every word to memory. When the day finally arrived, I borrowed Tim's tan blazer and white turtleneck and stood in front of the mirror in my room. Aside from the fact that Tim's clothes swallowed me whole, I looked pretty darn good. And I was ready.

Trina and I loaded into her 1977 black Monza, which she had paid for with money from her job at Dog n Suds. It had set her back $1,150.43, which she reminded us every time we got her floor mats dirty or didn't seem grateful for her driving us places.

We pulled into Windsor Elementary and parked the car. I stared down at the sheet music in my lap. My nerves were kicking in. Trina pulled the keys from the ignition, turned in her seat to face me, and said, "You're gonna do great, Matt. Let's get you in there."

The school cafeteria had been transformed. It was amazing what a bunch of streamers and the absence of a few lunch ladies had done for the place. As parents and teachers began filling the room, I felt overwhelmed by the growing size of the event.

All the contestants sat in a long row of folding chairs near the front of the cafeteria. I could see Trina standing in back. When it was my turn to sing, I stepped onto the stage and approached the microphone.

What I hadn't expected was a connection with the people who sat before me. I was only ten years old, but as I sang, something mystical passed between us.

> *You know I can't smile without you;*
> *I can't smile without you.*
> *I can't laugh and I can't sing;*
> *I'm finding it hard to do anything.*
> *You see, I feel sad when you're sad;*
> *I feel glad when you're glad.*
> *If you only knew what I'm going through.*
> *I just can't smile without you.*[2]

They didn't know what I was going through at home or in my basement, nor did I know what they were going through. But I felt as though I could see into them, and they into me. Something greater was in the room.

When the song was over, I heard their applause, but I only wanted to find my sister. I won't forget her taking my face in her hands, leaning in close, and saying, "That was unbelievable. I didn't know you could sing like that. I'm so proud of you."

I didn't win the talent show that night—actually the principal's daughter did. She tap-danced wearing half a tuxedo and sang "The Rainbow Connection." It had drawn very little applause except from our principal who clapped as if he had four arms. But none of that mattered to me because on the way home, my sister affirmed me. She told me all I could do with my music, encouraging me to play an instrument and get involved with a choir. She was my biggest cheerleader. I looked up to her in every way imaginable.

She was infinite.

Trina began watching for audition flyers for musicals with our community theater. She drove me from audition to audition. I cared less about my singing than I did about her dedication to who she believed I was. In her constant affirmation, she was singing my song—a song that identified me alone, a song that would never leave me, a song that would never change.

I had no idea what God had begun the night I sang at the talent show, but after graduating college, I began what has now been a twenty-year career, singing songs about God before groups of people—songs about his love, grace, and faithfulness. Some of the songs were bad, filled with clichés and overly simplistic answers to questions that might never be answered, but other songs have been powerful. I've witnessed their words and melodies finding a place in people's hearts—not answering their questions but affirming a presence greater than themselves.

I've never seen myself as a worthy representative of God because too much happened to me as a child, and my doubt has often left me feeling entirely inadequate. Oh, there are times I fully expect people to find out the truth about me: that I'm a fraud. And maybe it's true—maybe I *am* damaged goods. Maybe I'm the same as Keegan and my only rescue is to be so wrapped up with God that my whole life belongs to him—that even in my vocation, I would need to be directing people to something greater, even when I wasn't sure if that something greater was real.

Could it be that for all the darkness within me, and for all the brokenness, that instead of answering my questions, God put his song of dark *and* light in me and I've been singing it all this time—singing the song I was always meant to sing? A song that's honest and raw. A song of healing and pain. A song of love and hate. A song of hope and a song of doubt.

The book *A Prayer for Owen Meany* couldn't possibly open any more beautifully: "If there were no room for doubt, there would be no room for me."[3]

My doubt, my questions, and even my unbelief are a part of who God created me to be. I once felt so ashamed of them. But I believe that God was no more pleased the day I heard his voice calling out to me from the corn in Westfield than he was the day he stood in the doorway of my broken heart and was turned away because I couldn't bear his darkness.

He wasn't worried, upset, or offended that I turned him out into the cold. And because he waited on me to work out my faith (and doubt) with fear and trembling, eventually I started to believe again—to trust that the fingerprints on all the things I had collected in my jar really did belong to God.

Once upon a time, I walked away from the faith I knew, and I'm glad I did. I closed the door until I was ready for something more—for something greater. Passing through darkness will always be a part of life because trouble will always be with us. But as I strain my eyes amidst the shifting shadows, I find Jesus in silhouette. Every detail of his face is not recognizable, but his form is unmistakable.

I was ready to open the door. I only needed to let him know.

"Behold," I told him, "if once again you will stand at the door of my heart and knock, then I will take the chain from off the door."

THE QUIET HUM
My Life for the Glory of God

Out of suffering have emerged the strongest souls; the
most massive characters are seared with scars.
—Kahlil Gibran

During World War II, Nazi Germany was intent on emptying Europe of its Jewish population by either expulsion or genocide. This initiative was known as the Final Solution.

Irena Sendler, a small Polish Catholic woman, smuggled children and babies out to safety from the Warsaw Ghetto in Warsaw, Poland. She would come into the city masquerading as a plumber and on her way out place babies in a hidden compartment in the bottom of her toolbox or smuggle them out in gunnysacks. She did all of this right under the nose of her enemy. She saved twenty-five hundred children and infants before being caught, severely beaten, and imprisoned by Nazi guards. Sentenced to death, Irena would eventually be freed and remain in hiding until the end of the war.

Ms. Sendler wrote the name of each child she rescued on a piece of tissue paper and placed it in a jar, which she kept buried under an apple tree in her backyard. Her hope was to one day reunite each child rescued with his or her parents. But that reuniting barely happened at all, as only 1 percent of Jews in the Warsaw Ghetto survived. Most were sent to an extermination camp in Treblinka, where they were murdered in a gas chamber; others were killed in the Warsaw Ghetto Uprising. Ultimately, the war orphaned nearly every child Irena Sendler smuggled out from the Warsaw Ghetto.

My wife's very first struggle to understand God was when she learned about the Holocaust in elementary school. When we are old enough to take in the breadth of the Holocaust, doubt is a natural response. In many of our religious circles, we are told, "You just have to trust him." But there are times when we can no more trust God than we can trust Hitler, not that he is expecting us to.

There are times when doubting God's existence or his involvement in our lives is appropriate and perhaps even the right thing to do. Walking through life blindly as if the bad things that have happened have no bearing on our faith does not make us *more* faithful but brings to light our incapacity to sympathize with the suffering of others. This lack of empathy exposes a juvenile faith—an adolescent belief in God as our real Savior. Our "ignorance is bliss" approach, in which God is delivering us from evil only by "saving our souls," is a black eye on our faith that must be set right.

Our pursuit to understand why pain has created its own Treblinka death camp in our souls—stealing our children from us, bringing disease upon our physical bodies, allowing our sound minds to atrophy in the presence of mental illness—is a necessary part of our journey if we are ever to move our faith from adolescence into adulthood.

God has given each of us a pardon for our imprisoned doubt, and when we let ourselves off the hook and embrace our doubt, we are often propelled forward, closer to God than we ever thought possible. Searching for an answer, desiring an answer, does not make us faithless but rather shows our true identity, which is children of God doing what children do best: asking, "Why?"

The social-psychological phenomenon called the bystander effect, or bystander apathy, was first documented when Kitty Genovese was stabbed to death in the borough of Queens, New York, in 1964. It was reported that many neighbors heard her and that several even saw her being attacked but did nothing. Her attacker, Winston Moseley, fled the scene when someone called out to him from the street. Kitty, still alive, dragged herself to the back of her apartment building, but no one came for her. Ten minutes later, Moseley returned to finish the job, stabbing and raping her for another thirty minutes until she was dead. Only after it was over did anyone call for an ambulance.

The bystander effect might feel unlikely in this day of neighborhood watches and crime prevention initiatives, but there is bystander apathy within us all. We know of those who have been through metaphorical or even literal stabbings and beatings, or we have experienced the brutalities of life ourselves. We have faced trials of many kinds, but many of us have shelved them, not allowing God to use them for the good of others. And by denying the world access to our stories, we are living out the bystander effect by failing to realize how our pain could—how our stories just might …

set someone else free.

We come into contact with suffering people every day: who have been to hell and back, who wonder if God is a myth and are torn by the thought of it, whose marriages are hanging by a thread, whose kids have disabilities, whose hearts have been coarsened by the brutality of abuse, who can't manage to get out of bed because of the great depression. And when we don't understand our stories, when we don't *tell* our stories, we are no different than the people of Queens, New York, who left Kitty Genovese for dead.

It is noted in psychological journals regarding the bystander effect that when more witnesses are present during an assault, the victim is less likely to receive help. But when there are fewer witnesses or even just one, the chance of that witness coming to the victim's rescue increases dramatically. This is called the burden of responsibility.

Irena Sendler stood four feet eleven inches tall. When she began her mission, she stood alone because everyone else was too afraid to make the first move. You might be the only person in your family willing to expose the lies and tell the truth, and that may scare you to death. But the chances of someone being rescued, even in future generations, are far greater when people are willing to step out on their own. Because of your strength to step up to the plate, because of your courage to stand alone and honor the pain, because of your willingness to carry the burden of responsibility, the chance that others will be rescued has just increased dramatically.

———————

Remember Marcia Schwartz, our groundskeeper? From the time she was a little girl until her mother passed away, she prayed for her mother's release from mental illness. Her prayers were answered when her mom was eighty years old. She was cured just long enough to pray with Marcia and, for the first time, believe that something greater was out there and that this Something Greater was finally calling her home.

Out of the core wound of Marcia's faithful prayers for her mother's sanity came the calling to pray for others. Undoubtedly it would've been easier to ignore the pain—to forgo the calling God placed on her life. Thankfully she didn't, because all the people she has prayed for over the years have in some way been changed because of Marcia's faith.

But don't miss the true beauty of her story: how her sacrifice to petition God on our behalf is wrapped up in dark and light, good and evil, hope and fear, faith and doubt.

It is nearly incomprehensible that Marcia was willing to surrender herself to the mystery of a God who would heal her mom for only three short weeks after *forty years* of ceaseless prayers—a God she still believes is good.

I know. I don't get it either. But we don't have to. Only Marcia does. It is between her and God.

Marcia still has her bucket of name tags she's found orphaned around the parking lot, strewn across the church lawn over the years. And I imagine Irena Sendler still has her jar, filled with the names of every baby and child she saved, and carries it around with her in heaven.

And I have my jar too. Marcia's bucket of name tags is in it, and so is Irena Sendler, as both of these women remind me of the great hope we have that the lost orphans who are strewn across this world can be found. In our pain we are all orphans in some way because this world is not our home. It was never meant to be.

The day Becky took a handful of pills, she was an orphan of this world for sure. And although it may seem obvious that she took her own life, I'd like to think God smuggled her out of this world right under the nose of her enemy. And it wouldn't surprise me at all to find out that God has his own special jar and that Becky is kept safely within it, carried close to his side.

"So heaven is real and death is a lie."

The day I received the pen at Becky's funeral, I was reminded of just how personal and poetic God is. "Please write beautiful, hope-filled words," John told me—or God had. Becky's pen is perhaps the loveliest and most awful gift I have ever received. It is a broken-down treasure I couldn't possibly cherish any more than I do—a reminder that I have a job to do—a calling to tell my story.

But her pen wasn't passed on only to me; it was passed on to you as well so that your story could do a swan dive right into the hearts of the unredeemed, illuminating their darkness, promising them hope, and changing their story by helping them find God in the ruins.

Each of us has a calling that comes from the core ache within us—a calling to write with our lives the beautiful stories of God's redemption. To remind others that all of our pain has been regulated. So when hopelessness seems to have had the last word, the love of God instead, which has been written on our hearts, will set God's redemption loose in the enemy's pawnshop.

Our stories written out for the unredeemed. My life for the glory of God.

When I was a child, so many of the songs we sang in church meant nothing to me because I didn't understand their cadence or verbiage. But the third verse of the old hymn "The Love of God" was always perfectly clear to me:

Could we with ink the ocean fill,
And were the skies of parchment made;
Were every stalk on earth a quill,
And every man a scribe by trade;
To write the love of God above
Would drain the ocean dry;
Nor could the scroll contain the whole,
Though stretched from sky to sky.[1]

Like C. S. Lewis, I don't believe hell is a very large place. I agree that you could probably fit the entirety of it within a crack in the sidewalk. But there are times when its fury is unleashed into our world and our spirits deflate like balloons. In the chaos of fragmented lives so loud and garish, there is a quiet hum neatly folded and lying on our pillows. In the stillness of that hum, I believe that God is waiting. Why he waits in the quiet, we'll never know, but I believe he is there just the same.

For those of you who have lived your life beneath the overpass of life, waiting for something *un*painful to happen, I hope you will eventually curl up in your sleeping bag with God—that he'll stroke your hair and whisper all the things you *really* are right into your ear as you fall asleep. And with traffic raging all around you, I pray that you will hear only the quiet hum.

But oh God, for those who have never heard the quiet hum—the unfortunate ones who aren't capable of managing life, through no fault of their own—I believe they will find their peace. I believe that in the moment their souls fly off to the heavens, you will take them by the hand and lead them to a beautiful shore. And in white robes, before they do one other thing, each one who couldn't find their way will kneel down at that shoreline, and all of their demons will drink from an ocean of your grace, until there is nothing left of them.

Until there is nothing left of the unredeemed.

AFTERWORD

P.S. Over the last year, Becky's pen has never been far from me while writing this book, so it just felt "right" to transcribe this postscript by hand, with her pen, knowing that even in death, her life is being transferred to us in some small way.

Just a couple of weeks ago, on the evening of our twentieth wedding anniversary, Heather and I were sitting in a beautiful restaurant, celebrating our journey together. Out of nowhere she asked if I'd ever wished I hadn't gone through what I had as a child. At first I had trouble answering her question because if the pain goes away, so do the redemptive ways God showed up in my pain. If the horror stories go away, so does the God who comes to me from within the corn of Westfield. If the insecurity that has plagued me from the sexual brokenness of my childhood goes away, so does the sweet bearded substitute teacher who showed me the unconditional love of God. If Stepdad from Hell goes away, so does the feeling that God himself is proud of me and has adopted me as a son.

I'm not saying I wouldn't have wanted a pristine childhood, but if I had to trade the beautiful and peculiar ways God has shown up to get my attention, if I had to trade my capacity to have an eternal gaze, if I had to give up my ability to speak on behalf of the broken and torn as a result of my pain, if I had to trade my music, my hope, my uniqueness - if I had to exchange all of these beautiful things for a childhood void of abuse and exploitation, I don't know that I would.

And if that's true, haven't these unredeemed things, at least in some way, been redeemed? Haven't the sands of love been sifted heavier than those of the ruined potpourri of my unanswered prayers? And isn't my brokenness finally closer to heaven than hell?

My pain is not all gone, that's for sure. The "healing waters" have certainly not washed it away completely. But something greater has come my way, and somewhere along my journey that Something Greater has become more powerful within me than ruined scenes of my life.

The pen in my hand once scrawled out a hopeless woman's last words. I've called it the loveliest and most awful gift I've ever received. In the same way, these ruined scenes have become that too. They are a broken-down treasure I couldn't possibly cherish any more than I do. I wouldn't take anything for them. They have made me who I am.

For a year now, on every bike ride and every silent drive in my car, I've had butterflies in my stomach. I've hoped and prayed that this book would be a great help to you as you connect the dots of your life, redeemed or otherwise, back to God. I have prayed a thousand prayers on your behalf (and so has Marcia, by the way) that you would know that he is good and that he's God; that he is wonderful and terrible, big and small, gentle and hard, light and dark; that he is dangerously safe, mysteriously down-to-earth, intricately simple, effortlessly problematic, unquestionably questionable, life-giving and suffocating, an impossible houseguest, yet impossible to live without.

At the end of the day, though we remain uncertain of the mysterious ways of God, I believe that if we listen closely for his voice, more than anything else we will hear it just behind us, saying,

Me encanta. Me encanta. Me encanta.

I love,
Matt

DISCUSSION QUESTIONS

CHAPTER 1: THE PEN

1. What would you say to people like Tim and Janese, whose son committed suicide? What do you think God says to them?

2. Talk about a simplistic answer to a difficult question about God or life that negatively affected or distorted your view of God.

3. Has the phrase "God will use your pain and tragedy for his glory" ever bothered you? After giving it some thought, does it bother you now? If so, in what way?

4. What do you think about the possibility that the weak, hurting, and abused have been put in your life to help you rather than so you could help them?

5. How does the word *redemption* need its own personal redemption in your life?

For Personal Reflection

1. How might you have written your "own version of Christianity" and made Christianity or Christians seem irrelevant or perhaps even cruel to others?

2. Psalm 37:5 says, "Commit thy way unto the LORD; trust also in him; and he shall bring it to pass" (KJV). Is there a part of you that feels God owes you a life free from tragedy and pain? How much pain is acceptable?

3. Is the idea of diffusing your painful experiences rather than making them disappear altogether a reasonable goal for dealing with your pain? Spend some time visualizing what it looks like to live with pain but not having it control or dominate your life.

CHAPTER 2: ONE-SIDED PRAYERS

1. When did you first realize that not all of your prayers would be answered? How did you respond to this concept? What is your current response?

2. C. S. Lewis said, "I know now, Lord, why you utter no answer. You are yourself the answer. Before your face questions die away."[1] I personally find this quote difficult to grasp. Would you say your questions have "died away"? If so, explain.

3. If you were God, how would you respond differently than he did to the prayers of his people? How might you respond the same?

4. Sayings such as "When God closes a door, he opens a window" and "Everything happens for a reason" help some people remain positive during the normal frustrations and letdowns of life. In the wrong context, how have spiritual clichés such as these become destructive and created distance between God and his people?

For Personal Reflection

1. Think about this idea for a moment: "Unexpressed doubt can be toxic." Do you have serious doubts that have gone unexpressed? How have those doubts become toxic in your life?

2. This chapter talks about not feeling the need to protect God's reputation—that if God comes off as a liar because the promises in his Word have fallen short, so be it. In light of Psalm 37:4 ("Take delight in the LORD, and he will give you the desires of your heart"), how might you be protecting God's reputation in ways that are not helpful or honest?

As a side note, if you begin typing "Psalm 37" into Google, the drop-down will automatically display "Psalm 37:4." People really love this verse.

CHAPTER 3: THE CHAIN

1. Tell of some of the positive and negative messages you received about grace and salvation in your church of origin.

2. Briefly (so all can share) take a moment to tell the story of your initial conversion experience. What did it mean to you at the time?

3. How has your understanding of salvation changed over the years?

4. Have you ever kicked God out of your life for a time? If so, looking back, how do you think kicking God out of your life might have helped you move forward in your spiritual journey?

For Personal Reflection

1. If you are a believer, think back to your initial conversion experience. Re-create the scene in your mind. Where were you? Who did you pray with? Or did you simply raise your hand? Some people have a life-altering, 180-degree shift in their lives after making a decision to follow Jesus. How did your life change after your initial conversion?

2. Are there questions you've been holding on to for years (or even decades) that you've never felt permitted to ask God? Are there things you've wanted to say to God but were afraid doing so might cause you to lose your salvation? What would it feel like to get to an honest place with God where you could finally say the things you've needed to say?

CHAPTER 4: THE AGE OF RECKONING

1. When was your age of reckoning—the time in your life when denial stopped working and you struggled to manage the pain that was secretly hidden away?

2. What is your personal drug of choice—the "worthless idol" you use to avoid *real* life (food, shopping, control, exercise, sex, alcohol, prescription drugs, pornography, cutting, video games, sleep, even church/God/spirituality)?

3. What are some of your character defects?

4. Is there a part of your life that you fear is already hardened plastic? Talk about what it is and why you don't think it's salvageable.

5. What does the phrase "It's painful before it's peaceful" mean to you? Try to remember a change that was painful to make but brought more peace into your life.

For Personal Reflection

1. Jonah 2:8 says, "Those who cling to worthless idols forfeit the grace that could be theirs" (NIV 1984). What do you think are some of those graces in life that could be yours?

- Fully engaging with your children, spouse, friends, or coworkers

- Being involved in extracurricular activities you've
  always wanted to try
- Having peace and joy in your everyday life

2. "You cannot solve an internal problem with an external solution."
What does this mean to you? Take time to think about a deeper issue
you'd like to fix. How have you tried to fix it externally? What would
it look like to go after it internally?

3. If you are ready to address your core wound, write down what you
think it might be. At some point, speak your core wound out loud to
God and to a friend you can trust.

CHAPTER 5: PUT AWAY THE GLITTER

1. Take a moment to think about how the story of Noah's ark, the
greatest God-massacre of all time, covers the walls of Christian
day-care centers and church nurseries. What are some other ways
Christendom has sprinkled glitter in places it doesn't belong?

2. "When our faith is built upon a theology of no more pain, we fail
to hold dark and light together and cannot experience the fullness of
God." In what ways do you feel you might not be experiencing the
fullness of God?

3. What are some ways God has created dark and light in your life?

4. Have you ever had it out with God? Explain.

For Personal Reflection

> I form the light and create darkness,
>> I bring prosperity and create disaster;
>> I, the LORD, do all these things. (Isa. 45:7)

1. How does the Isaiah scripture sit with you? Remember, God is not afraid of you. He welcomes your honesty.

2. If God pulled up a chair before you, looked directly into your eyes, and asked you to tell him the truth about how you feel (or have felt) about him, would you feel secure enough to be brutally honest? If so, what would you say? It might be time to get out a journal and write down exactly how you feel.

CHAPTER 6: THE FAMILY WAY

1. There are subjects we've all been brought up not to talk about—taboo issues that make us uncomfortable. Incest is definitely one of those subjects. What are a few others, and why do you think they make people uneasy?

2. Jesus is the truest example of one who didn't flinch in the face of evil—the evil we participated in or the evil that happened to us. In his encounter with the woman at the well, he was not a bit squeamish or uncomfortable. In the way that Jesus was safe company for the hurting, how are you a safe place for those with a backstory involving taboo issues?

3. "God's own story was full of disorder, his past every bit as messed up as mine. And when God saw how out of control things had gotten, he sent his Son to clean things up. If God's past mattered that much to him, I figured mine mattered too." How do you feel about this statement from chapter 6?

4. What do you believe holds people back from investigating their pasts with full abandon? Now get personal: What holds *you* back?

For Personal Reflection

Time magazine published an article many years ago called "Why We Get Disgusted."[2] The article mentioned a concept called touch transference, which is the belief that when something disgusting is introduced by touch to something wholesome, it makes that wholesome thing less desirable.

This theory was tested by loading grocery carts with food items and then placing desired items in close proximity to products such as toilet paper. The study revealed that when desired items were placed near the undesirables, people no longer preferred those items as they once had. And if the undesirable items were in transparent packaging, the desirables were even less desirable.

1. After reflecting on this information, consider those stories that involve ruin at a deeper level than most of us are comfortable with. How do you think we can overcome our inability to sit with someone else's story as it is?

2. Maybe your story is one that will make others uncomfortable. Although you trust that no part of your story could ever make God squeamish, are there parts of your story you've never told because you've felt you would be judged or thought less of? If so, take a few minutes to consider whether it's time to share your full story, and if you feel it *is* time, make sure you do so with someone you trust implicitly. Do not begin by going public on Facebook, a blog, or another social media platform.

3. Take time to reflect on this thought from Dan Allender:

> It is out of our wounds, from the core ache within
> us, that we find our calling.

How might this be true for you?

CHAPTER 7: AND WEE DANCED

1. Talk about a time when you were desperate to hear from God and he fell silent. In what ways did this challenge or hurt your faith?

2. We will never know why God allows for suffering. Some say it's a consequence of the fall. Others, such as C. S. Lewis, say pain is God's "megaphone to rouse a deaf world."[3] What do you think?

3. I mentioned having made a demand of God when I told him to go ahead and heal my sister. Does this kind of demand seem like a

temper tantrum, or would you consider it to be putting one's hope in God? Have you ever made a demand of God? Why or why not?

For Personal Reflection

1. "Hope is creative and so resourceful. It can take thumbtacks and tape and stick things back together if we'll let it. Hope survives." Think of a situation in which you've given up hope. Consider whether this suspension of hope is helping or hurting your faith.

2. Moses was able to convince God to change his mind, as was Amos. Most of us have learned to pray, "God, change me" or "God, change my heart." What would it be like to pray "God, change," instead?

Take a few minutes to see if something you'd like to change God's mind on comes to your attention. If so, write it down and then come back to it later in the week and consider praying it boldly.

CHAPTER 8: LOVE SIFTING

1. How do you feel about the Robert Farrar Capon quote, especially the line "Evil is where we meet God"?

2. Often in times of great tragedy or loss, it seems as if God shows up unannounced in ways we don't expect. I don't believe these times are coincidental. How has God showed up for you in the middle of a tragic experience?

3. "There are moments, in the company of those who care, when it feels as if a huge minus sign has replaced the division sign and our burdens aren't being divided at all; they're being subtracted." Can you think of a time in your life when it made no sense that you should be at peace but somehow you were? Explain.

For Personal Reflection

1. "All of the good in my life has a contrast," my friend Kara told us in chapter 5. "So when the contrast comes, I plop myself down in the middle of the pain, frustration, or unmet expectations and I wait on God." For me, Ellen was God's showing up, his comfort on full display.

Spend a few moments remembering times when God showed up for you. Commit these to memory so you can return to them when you are struggling through a difficult time.

2. It's easy to get caught up in life and not take time to engage in what God might be doing all around us. Some people keep a journal to look back and recount the ways God has shown up for them. What could you do to be more aware of God's handiwork in your life?

CHAPTER 9: ME TOO

1. Your church of origin might have presented an image of God that was simplistic and easy to understand. This view leaves people with

the impression that life should also be easy to manage. How have these messages made you feel alone or brought on shame when you couldn't overcome a particular sin or difficult situation?

2. Why do people with more difficult life circumstances keep their distance from other believers or from God?

3. How do you feel about the idea that God's power is made *perfect* in our weakness? Is this a message you understood in your church of origin?

4. C. S. Lewis said, "Friendship … is born at the moment when one man says to another 'What! You too? I thought that no one but myself …'" How are you this kind of person to people? What are some ways you could take it even further?

For Personal Reflection

1. Let's revisit the phrase "I will *glory* in my weakness." On a personal level, what do these words mean to you? How have you integrated this practice into your life by sharing your weaknesses with others?

2. Without an ounce of self-condemnation, do your best to answer this question: Who specifically is benefiting from the painful lessons you have learned in your life? Are you finding (or missing) opportunities in your everyday life to say "me too" to those who express their personal struggles or grief to you?

CHAPTER 10: ME ENCANTA

1. We've been told all our lives that God is love. Some experience that love in nature, with their children or partner, through Scripture, or in doing what they love to do. Talk about one specific way in which you almost always experience God's love.

2. Have you ever had what you might call "a heavenly encounter" with God—an unexpected and tangible visit from him you couldn't deny? How did that change your view of God?

3. What does the phrase "Sometimes it feels as if God has invited himself into *my pain*, when I had hoped to be invited into *his healing*" mean to you?

4. As we grow into spiritual adulthood, we begin to have new insights about who God is. At some point, a theology of "God is good all the time" will be challenged by the harsh reality of painful life circumstances, which is a natural and healthy part of growing with him. How would you say your image of God has changed as you've matured spiritually?

For Personal Reflection

1. Take a few moments to think about what life is like when you are going through a difficult time. Why are we so eager, even desperate, to punctuate our pain before it's time? Why are we unwilling to leave an ellipsis where an ellipsis belongs?

2. Take some time to write down the undeniable ways you've felt God's presence. It could have happened while gardening, listening to music, enjoying your dog, working out, watching a movie, or experiencing the birth of a child or the death of a loved one. These are the times we must cling to when life feels hopeless or even Godless. We cannot always live on the mountaintop, but we can look back on these transcendent moments with God and let them renew our faith.

CHAPTER 11: THE UNTOLD STORY—I USED TO BE MATT PETRINO

1. Sometimes we work hard to keep things presentable on the outside, especially when we are struggling with what's broken on the inside. Describe a way you present yourself that isn't completely authentic.

2. Are you ever afraid that one day, without warning, you will completely lose it, go off the deep end, and do permanent damage to your family or relationships? How does this lie feel grounded in reality? How would God respond to the notion that we have little or no say over our future?

3. Do you really believe that people can change? Talk about a person who, against the odds, changed his or her life for the better.

4. How have *you* changed? Have you survived something that you should commend yourself for?

For Personal Reflection

1. The statement "We may not live in the past, but the past lives in us" stopped me the first time I heard it. Write down one or two ways you believe that your past still influences who you are.

2. I have a friend who says of his stress, "It's coming out sideways," meaning he is either road raging or yelling at flight attendants when his anger is actually about something else. Think about a time when your untold story pushed its way into your life without permission. What were some of the symptoms? For me, it was abusing alcohol and minimizing problems that I needed to take more seriously. What about you?

CHAPTER 12: DEFAULT SETTINGS

1. A distinction between "glass half-full" and "glass half-empty" personalities is made in this chapter. Many of our character traits seem to be imbedded into our genetic makeup. How have you felt pressure to change this part of your God-given personality?

2. "Change is most definitely a good thing, but at some point we need to close the 'alternate settings' tab before we check every item on the list and give ourselves the kind of false hope that can become destructive." How do you feel about this statement?

3. What are some unrealistic expectations you've had concerning your "default settings"? What are some unrealistic expectations you've had

for the "default settings" of your partner, best friend, children, or coworkers?

4. You might not be able to change the beginning of your story, but you can change the present way you are living as well as the end of your story. How do you feel about changing directions in your life? Is it time to fully accept the past so you can move forward in life?

For Personal Reflection

1. In *The Message*, Matthew 5:5 says we can be "content" with ourselves, exactly as we are, and that we are "blessed" when we do. Take some time to consider whether or not you are content with who you are at this very moment.

2. Accepting ourselves is hard work when there are things we'd still like to change. A toddler certainly needs to become less stubborn, but we wouldn't love that toddler any less if he didn't. How can you apply this same principle to yourself? Do you have a gracious and loving attitude toward yourself? Write down some things about yourself that do *not* need to change.

CHAPTER 13: SOMEONE ELSE'S STORY

1. What scenes from your childhood have you edited to make them more palatable either for yourself or for others?

2. What scenes from your childhood have you censored from your story, cutting them out completely?

3. Think about the part of your story you have never told. You don't have to tell it now, but at least tell the group if there *is* a story you've never told. You can say, "I don't want to talk about it right now, but there is something I've never told anyone." Start there.

4. Anne Lamott says, "You own everything that happened to you. Tell your stories ... If people wanted you to write warmly about them, they should've behaved better." Often we feel indebted to protect our family members by keeping the family secrets. How have you done this in your life?

For Personal Reflection

1. "Where there's pain, there's a wound." Let that sink in for a few minutes. If we have an external wound, we go to the clinic, we see a doctor, we dress and care for the wound. How have you neglected to care for your internal wounds?

2. Brennan Manning says, "In a futile attempt to erase our past, we deprive the community of our healing gift. If we conceal our wounds out of fear and shame, our inner darkness can neither be illuminated nor become a light for others." You might have a burning desire to make a difference in the kingdom of God. How do you respond to the idea that your story is what God will use most of all? Take some

time to think about any missed opportunities you've had to tell your story to someone who needed to hear it.

CHAPTER 14: REDEEMED 2.0

1. The phrase "God works in mysterious ways" sounds a little like this scripture from Romans:

> How great are [God's] wisdom and knowledge and riches! How impossible it is for us to understand his decisions and his methods! (Rom. 11:33 TLB)

What does this passage mean to you?

2. "We need for [the mystery of God] to be appropriated in a way that is accessible to our understanding. We need to make sure it doesn't butt up against our theology or ideology in a way that makes God look foolish—so *we* don't look foolish." Taking into account this passage from the book, consider how theology has taken precedence over the mystery of God. Although we cannot be driven by our hearts alone, we also cannot put all our trust in the conventional wisdom of man. How do we find a balance between these two?

3. Have you ever felt as if your life is being scrutinized or found yourself under the watchful eye of someone who seemed to have it all together? What was that like?

4. Often we judge the lives or choices of others, but having grace for them means God will have grace for us. Where do you think *your* life would be without God's redemption?

For Personal Reflection

1. We often rest on our own strength, talent, or aptitude as the source of our redemption. We spin our wheels trying to figure things out. But trusting our own wisdom is not always a good thing. Speaking directly to those who were relying too much on conventional wisdom, the apostle Paul said, "God chose the foolish things of the world to shame the wise; God chose the weak things of the world to shame the strong" (1 Cor. 1:27). How might the weak and foolish things of this world be used to expose your own personal weaknesses?

2. Brené Brown says, "The people who have a strong sense of love and belonging believe they are worthy of love and belonging." Consider whether you feel worthy to have your deepest hurt, fear, or loss redeemed by God. Do you have a vision for what that might look like?

CHAPTER 15: BROTHELS AND BASEMENTS

1. For some, being redeemed or receiving love can be painful and even agonizing if it isn't something they received as a child. Do you think there's validity to this statement? Why or why not?

2. Does your church or faith community feel like a safe place to sift through your personal hurts, grievances with God, or most haunting questions about life? What would a "safe faith community" look like? How can you be a safe place for others?

3. In Psalm 44, King David (also known as "a man after God's own heart") called God a liar and a cheat and even blamed God for his difficult life circumstances. Have you ever given yourself permission to take God to task for what felt like his absence (or even his testing) at a particularly dark time in your life?

4. We often think of the Son of God going to a cross to suffer for our sins as an event that is now in the past. But what if every time we suffer, God is suffering right alongside us? How does this change your perception of God's compassion toward us?

For Personal Reflection

1. Take a moment to think about people you know who have had abusive or problematic backstories. Just as God was there when these things were happening to them, how could you also be present for them as they grieve? Write down their names and commit to reaching out to them in the coming weeks.

2. Let's consider that whole King David thing again. In anger, David told God exactly how he felt about him, yet we tend to be fairly well behaved when it comes to being angry with God. This position may not be helping us deepen our faith. In fact, the opposite could

be true. "In some ways it is devastating to tell God all you wish he had done differently, saved you from, or converted you into… But maybe the moment you flip God the bird is the exact moment he looks into your eyes and says, 'Well done, my good and faithful servant.'" How do you respond to this? Is there something you might need to forgive God for in order to move your relationship with him to a deeper level? What is holding you back?

CHAPTER 16: MELODY UNCHAINED

1. If there were a song that identified the essence of who you are, what would that song sound like? (Let the artists in your group help get this question off the ground.)

2. How would the world be a different place if when people screwed up or lived apart from God's love, we sang their songs and reminded them who they really are?

3. Because God's ways are higher than ours, we will never fully comprehend his song. How can we live with the tension of God's song when it never seems to resolve?

4. "God has not always caused our pain, but he has *always* allowed for it. That's the hard truth. Harder still is that we don't know why." After spending some time with this book, would you say you feel the same about a quote like this? If not, explain what has changed.

For Personal Reflection

1. "There comes a point in our lives when either we will believe in a higher power or we won't. It is simply a question we all must answer for ourselves. *Is there more?*" Do you believe there is more? Give yourself permission to answer this question honestly. If the answer is "No, I don't think there is more" or "I'm really not sure," make it a point to share this information with someone who is safe.

2. If we are honest with ourselves, the hard truth is that many of us have yet to find answers to very difficult and legitimate questions. But beyond the answers to our questions, take some time to consider what it is you might *really* be searching for. Write down some ideas and then at some point this week, share them with a friend.

CHAPTER 17: THE QUIET HUM

1. Bystander apathy, which resulted in the death of Kitty Genovese, occurs when individuals do not offer help to a victim if other people are present. They bear no burden of responsibility because they expect others to step in and take care of it. How does this analogy parallel our spiritual lives?

2. Are you willing to reach out to those who are hurting, even if no one else does? If so, how? Is there a specific people group you feel most connected to, and does that in any way coincide with your core wound?

3. Take a moment to think about whether God's love has become greater than your pain, despair, or unanswered prayers. Is what you've been through worth what you've gained as a result of it? Would you say your pain has been redeemed, or is it still in the process of being redeemed?

For Personal Reflection

As this book study comes to a close, I want to thank you for hanging in there. My hope and prayer is that you will be a more effective and productive person of God. That said, I want to leave you with this question:

1. Marcia's calling to pray comes from the core ache of praying for her mother's mental illness. My calling to brokenness and recovery comes from the deep wounds of my childhood. Examine the things in your life you feel passionate about. Why are you passionate about them? Can you trace any of those passions back to the core ache (the pain or trauma) you've experienced in your life? If so, isn't it time to allow God to use the beautiful mixture of that pain and passion for his glory? Your life for the glory of God.

NOTES

CHAPTER 1: THE PEN

1. This is the author's personal definition.

CHAPTER 3: THE CHAIN

1. Anne Lamott, *Traveling Mercies: Some Thoughts on Faith* (New York: Pantheon, 1999), 50.

CHAPTER 4: THE AGE OF RECKONING

1. *Alcoholics Anonymous: The Big Book*, 4th ed., www.aa.org/assets/en_US/en_bigbook _chapt5.pdf, 58–59.

2. Susan Forward, quoted in "I'm Screaming—Are You Listening?" *Safe Relationships Magazine*, May 13, 2011, www.saferelationshipsmagazine.com/i'm-screaming-are -you-listening.

3. T. S. Eliot, "Little Gidding," *Four Quartets* (New York: Harcourt, Brace, 1943).

CHAPTER 5: PUT AWAY THE GLITTER

1. Indigo Girls, "Prince of Darkness," *Indigo Girls*, © 1989 Epic Records.

2. Richard Rohr, *Things Hidden: Scripture as Spirituality* (Cincinnati: St. Anthony Messenger Press, 2007), Kindle edition.

3. See *The Color Purple* (1985), IMDb Quotes, www.imdb.com/title/tt0088939/quotes.

CHAPTER 6: THE FAMILY WAY

1. Ian Morgan Cron, *Jesus, My Father, the CIA, and Me: A Memoir … of Sorts* (Nashville: Thomas Nelson, 2011), 47.

2. Dan Allender, "The Intersection of Character and Leadership," Willow Creek Association's 2002 Leadership Summit, Willow Creek Community Church, Chicago.

CHAPTER 7: AND WEE DANCED

1. C. S. Lewis, as portrayed in *Shadowlands*, directed by Richard Attenborough (1993; Hollywood, CA: HBO Home Video, 1999), DVD.

CHAPTER 8: LOVE SIFTING

1. Robert Farrar Capon, *The Romance of the Word: One Man's Love Affair with Theology* (Grand Rapids, MI: Eerdmans, 1995), 170; italics in the original.

CHAPTER 9: ME TOO

1. C. S. Lewis, *The Four Loves* (New York: Harcourt, Brace, 1960), 78.

2. Rainer Maria Rilke, *Letters to a Young Poet*, trans. Stephen Mitchell (New York: Vintage, 1986), 34–35.

CHAPTER 11: THE UNTOLD STORY—I USED TO BE MATT PETRINO

1. "Samuel Pisar Quotes," AZ Quotes, www.azquotes.com/quote/735131.

2. Elie Wiesel, quoted in Joseph Berger, "Man in the News; Witness to Evil: Eliezer Weisel, *New York Times*, October 15, 1986, nytimes.com/1986/10/15/world /man-in-the-news-witness-to-evil-eliezer-weisel.html.

CHAPTER 12: DEFAULT SETTINGS

1. Dolly Parton, interview by Queen Latifah, *The Queen Latifah Show*, Sony Pictures Television, October 21, 2013.

2. "Group Therapy," *Celebrity Rehab with Dr. Drew*, YouTube, www.vh1.com/shows /celebrity_rehab_with_dr_drew/group-therapy/604646/video/#id=1653802.

3. David Foster Wallace, in *Way More Than Luck: Commencement Speeches on Living with Bravery, Empathy, and Other Existential Skills* (San Francisco: Chronicle Books, 2015), 181.

4. Thomas Merton, "When in the Soul of the Serene Disciple."

CHAPTER 13: SOMEONE ELSE'S STORY

1. Anne Lamott's Facebook page, accessed October 30, 2015, www.facebook.com /AnneLamott/posts/156983721097946.

2. Matt Redman, "Blessed Be Your Name," *Where Angels Fear to Tread*, © 2002 Survivor Records.

3. Brennan Manning, *Abba's Child: The Cry of the Heart for Intimate Belonging* (Colorado Springs, CO: NavPress, 2002), 13.

4. "Clint Eastwood Quotes," BrainyQuote, www.brainyquote.com/quotes/quotes/c /clinteastw446715.html.

CHAPTER 14: REDEEMED 2.0

1. Phillips, Craig, and Dean, "Great I Am," *Breathe In*, © 2012 Fair Trade/Columbia.

2. Norah Jones, "Don't Know Why," *Come Away with Me*, © 2002 Blue Note.

3. Brené Brown, "The Power of Vulnerability," TED Talks, transcript, June 2010, www.ted.com/talks/brene_brown_on_vulnerability/transcript?language=en.

CHAPTER 15: BROTHELS AND BASEMENTS

1. Sherman Alexie, "What You Pawn I Will Redeem," *New Yorker*, April 21, 2003, www.newyorker.com/magazine/2003/04/21/what-you-pawn-i-will-redeem.

2. Matt Maher, "Empty and Beautiful," *Empty and Beautiful*, © 2008 Essential.

3. "Audre Lorde Quotes," Goodreads, www.goodreads.com/quotes/475771-wherever -the-bird-with-no-feet-flew-she-found-trees.

CHAPTER 16: MELODY UNCHAINED

1. Bryan Morse, "The God Molecule," *Bryan Morse's Blog*, www.bryanmorse.wordpress .com/2013/05/03/the-god-molecule/.

2. Barry Manilow, "Can't Smile Without You," *Even Now*, © 1978 Arista.

3. Frederick Buechner, quoted in John Irving, *A Prayer for Owen Meany* (New York: Garp Enterprises, 1989), 3.

CHAPTER 17: THE QUIET HUM

1. Frederick M. Lehman, "The Love of God," http://cyberhymnal.org/htm/l/o/loveofgo.htm.

DISCUSSION QUESTIONS

1. C. S. Lewis, *Till We Have Faces: A Myth Retold* (New York: Harcourt, 1980), 308.

2. Michael D. Lemonick, "Why We Get Disgusted," *Time*, May 24, 2007, http://content.time.com/time/magazine/article/0,9171,1625167,00.html.

3. C. S. Lewis, *The Problem of Pain* (New York: Macmillan, 1962), 81.

Dear Reader,

For those of you suffering through your own personal hell, fear may have you pinned up against the lockers, whispering into your ear, "If only people knew the truth about you..." But I believe we are only as sick as our secrets. And if that's true, maybe our healing, maybe the truth of who we really are, will be found when we gather the courage to tell our stories, to bear witness not only to life's difficulties but also to the amazing grace of God. My friends, I believe this is how we will change the broken spirit of humanity.

I'd like to personally invite you to join me on this beautiful journey of redemption.

Here's how to connect with me:

Blog: **www.mattbayswriter.com**

Twitter: **@mattbayswriter**

Facebook: **facebook.com/mattbayswriter**

Finding God in the Ruins music video:
bit.ly/matt-bays-videos